TALKING WITH TREES

THE ART OF THE DRUIDS CLEARLY EXPLAINED

DRUIDS WISDOM VOLUME 1

HAPPY PLANTS

FOR HAPPY

PEOPLE

BEN LINDEMANN

IN MEMORY OF HORST MARTIN

FOR ALL DRUIDS WHO HAVE BEEN

ARE

AND WILL BE

©BEN LINDEMANN 2019

ISBN: PAPERBACK: 978-3-7428-5606-9
HARDCOVER: 978-3-7428-5607-6
E-BOOK   978-3-7428-5608-3

ENGLISH TRANSLATION OF THE 3RD REVISED EDITION OF
"LINDEMANN, BEN: SPRECHEN MIT BÄUMEN 2013, BOD"

COVER DESIGN, PHOTOS, LAYOUT AND TYPESETTING: BEN LINDEMANN
TRANSLATION: JOHN WATERFIELD, BEN LINDEMANN

Contact: info@druidenwissen.ch

Website: http://www.druidenwissen.ch

More than just superstition

Much has been written about the effects and the being of trees. From the 'tree horoscope' to 'channelling the angelic beings of plants'. Some authors are evidently, or supposedly, getting into close contact with plants, or even regularly falling into a kind of connected trance. The methods they use are various: starting from ancient pujas to homespun sacrificial rituals of many different kinds and extending to purely imaginary 'tree tripping'. Likewise, the results vary, from your simple esoteric trip to a state of deep connection.

The ancient Celts saw it in a quite more pragmatic perspective. Druids communicated with trees just as a matter of course, and thereby acquired great wisdom. As a result, the entire Celtic culture was permeated with joy in life, confidence and a deep trust in life's eternal laws.

The aim of this book is to present the technique of communicating with trees which has been practically identical in all parts of Europe and Asia, so that anyone will be able to charge themselves with primordial energy and, with a little practice, get advice and help from our leafy companions. All you need for this is knowledge of the ancient method and a little practice. The techniques which are described here in simple terms, and their effects, have little or nothing to do with superstition or any kind of religious persuasion, but are intended for all those with open eyes and ears, who would like to walk life's winding road smiling and with a straight back. The path of the ancients not only permits us to communicate with trees. It also teaches us, irrespective of our world view or religion, a deeper understanding of ourselves and of the world we live in. It encourages us to develop patience and strengthens our trust and joy in life in a peaceful and persistent way.

But let's make a start – there's a new world out there waiting to be discovered!

Talking without mouth – Listening without ears

It is hardly likely that you will ever find yourself directly addressed by a tree – seeing that trees don't have a mouth for talking to us directly. All the same, from the dawn of time it was possible for the Druids to contact trees and actively exchange with them.

The abilities and basic techniques required for this are best learned step by step. One may need several months of practice, while another will get it on the very first day. The treasure of wisdom and personal counsel which then becomes accessible is truly inestimable. Depending on the sort, the location and the individual tree, they may be infinitely wise, loving and beneficent, though they can also be grumpy and recalcitrant.

When our human understanding and logical thinking fall short, the thoughts and images they communicate to us are very helpful.

Just to head off any unrealistic expectations – a tree neither is an omniscient oracle, nor is it a wishing well. 'Dear tree, please give me loads of money' is not an approach that will work. And there can also be situations where a tree just prefers to remain silent.

Perhaps for that very reason there are said to have been Druids, like the fabulous Merlin, who preferred the society of trees to that of human beings.

Who is a Druid?

Anyone who has read Asterix is familiar with the character Getafix, and therefore has a clear idea of what is to be expected of a Druid.
He has a long white beard, is exceedingly wise, cuts mistletoe with a golden sickle and concocts various magical potions. Nice but not quite true nowadays.

I am not concerned here to write yet another histological treatise about Celts and Druidry. In addition to Celtic sources, to get the whole picture I also draw on Germanic, Nordic and Indian ones.

The knowledge and philosophy that lies behind Druidism is actually primevally Indo-European in its roots, whether we are talking about Gaulish, Hibernian, Hyperborean or any other kind of Druid: when we refer in this book to Celts and Druids, we are not referring to a particular place or specific time frame.

Provided their effects prove beneficial, many quite new methods have won acceptance as well. From this perspective, some New Age believers and Neopagans can equally well be described in a loose sense as modern Druids. Their role models – the Druids of the Celtic tradition, the Indo-Germanic seers and oracles and the shamans of the Indian-Asiatic tradition would not be likely to take it amiss.

The idealised picture of a Druid is best summed up in the person of Merlin. He draws on the wisdom of nature and uses the powers he acquires wisely. For this he doesn't need a doctorate, or hierarchical rank of any kind – just open senses for perceiving the world around him openly and without prejudice.

Some thoughts about city Druids

Even trees along city streets and in parks can be exciting to talk to and can give you a lot of knowledge about sense and values illusiveness and life itself.

If it is impossible for you at the present time to access a tree directly, there is still a way you can communicate with it.

Even if you can't leave the house you are living in, it is still possible for you to visit a tree in thought. Try to get hold of a tree lexicon, ideally with good illustrations, and look at the photos of the trees depicted.

Just immerse yourself in the picture and try to put yourself completely into the location of the photographer or painter. What was the weather like, the wind, the sounds? What did the surroundings feel like in other ways? Try simply to merge with the picture. This works even with painted trees in books! In certain circumstances it is even sufficient if you close your eyes and picture a tree intensively in your mind's eye.

Later on, we will describe two other possible ways by which, with a bit of practice, you can link in with the power of trees.

Nonetheless direct contact makes a whole lot more sense, as then you won't have any external 'interference' jamming the signal, and the mutual pictures, feelings and concepts are also very much easier and clearer to perceive.

How to identify trees

Even an educated Druid can't possibly know every tree species from all over the world. Therefore, I would advise you to get hold of a tree reference book, ideally a well-illustrated one, for the region where you want to converse with trees. A pocket edition is quite sufficient for consulting when you are out walking. In botanical gardens you don't often need to look things up, as almost all the plants will be labelled. It is a good way of getting to know trees in an uncomplicated way, even if you live in the city. In the second and third parts of the book, we will introduce the being of trees and their likely characteristics in greater detail.

Communication by means of existing patterns

When a Druid talks to a tree, it's all pretty unspectacular to look at. First, he takes a deep look, then approaches the tree, perhaps looks around the landscape a bit, attends to noises and other sources of disturbance. When he feels the time is right, he moves into the zone between the crown and the rootstock, positions himself carefully (seated or standing), perhaps closes his eyes and waits in this attitude for a while. Inside him, however, a well-trained process is going on, one that is fundamentally different from the purely imaginative procedure commonly used in esoteric practice which relies on the person's own power of imagination.

After a certain period of preparation, which serves to calm and pacify his own conscious mind, the Druid opens up to the content of the tree's consciousness. This is because if we are to be capable of receiving an influence, we first have to tune our senses to it. In this way not just the ancient Druids, but anyone at all can communicate with the tree, through resonance in the form of feelings and emotions, and even in proper sentences.

Just as in a conversation between two humans, the tree can only make use of the feelings, emotions and language already present in its human counterpart.

The first time I talked to the mightiest kauri tree in New Zealand, a true wise archont of the kingdom of plants I was very surprised it could switch between English and German. In doing so it was just alternating between my linguistic sets, in keeping with my expectations.

Conversations with trees are usually very pleasant and extremely rewarding, though sometimes they can be serious and full of wise words of advice in a situation of need. A hazel bush will undoubtedly convey a different kind of conscious contents than a beech tree. It can only become threatening if you try to force a tree into dialogue against its will. From the birch to the yew, tree beings have one property in common: they like us, seeing us as children. That, incidentally, is how they refer to us as well – 'children' or 'the young folks'.

The nature of dryads
Human beings and animals possess a separate individual consciousness. Plants share a great part of their consciousness with all other members of the same species. This species awareness is generally distributed in a kind of dream state among all representatives of a genus.

The mightier the tree you visit, the more powerfully this consciousness will be awake in the tree itself. Though that shouldn't stop you talking to a sapling. It is just going to show you a quite different facet of the same consciousness.

Your experience will vary depending on the species, the individual tree, and the wood or the surroundings. Based on these factors, you can expect either a pleasant chat or gain profound lore and wisdom.

Every large wood will have one or more 'aspect trees', which are permanently in contact with the other trees of the wood and with neighbouring aspect trees of other wooded areas. You recognise them as being particularly powerful representatives of their species. Their task consists in representing the woodland network. If one of these trees is felled, it is a major loss, as one or more other, less experienced trees must then take on the role. If the wood is reduced by clearances, the powers of the aspect trees will be attenuated likewise, as they draw a large part of their power from the wood.

And then there are, quite different kinds of 'pixies' who can take up lodging in any tree. Once I was very surprised at the quite unserious character of a yew, which emanated a cheery faith in life in the most gleeful and light-hearted tones, all the while pretending to be 'the yew'. Then I spotted the little coal tit just over my head, visibly enjoying himself hopping up and down the branches. But unfortunately, its individual consciousness just prevented it going so far as to alight on me.

Compared with this, the fourth and last kind of consciousness you may find indwelling in a tree is rather unpleasant – lost souls, after having departed this earthly life, may occasionally miss the 'exit into the light' and obstinately, or mistakenly, take up residence in a tree before their final departure. The trees allow this, and after a period of tranquillisation do go on to release these poor souls into the light eventually. But today this is a very rare occurrence.

If completely different beings like sylphs, pixies or gnomes make their presence felt – well then, dear reader, you can count yourself lucky, because it doesn't happen often. – And please be modest and polite! Because they may be in a good mood, or then again, they may become hopping mad. But in that case your own imagination is probably playing tricks.

Trees, religion and mysticism

From the Siberian shamans to the Maoris of New Zealand practically all religions and cultures are based on a kind of mystical World Tree as a model and for purification and self-recognition.

The Nordic, Celtic, Jewish and even some Ancient Greek mystics know the world tree under the names of Yggdrasil, Irminsul, Cabala or simply 'World Tree'. In generally apocryphal myths, it represents an orientation framework for the different realms of the inner and outer cosmos. So, by a strange irony of fate, a World Tree can be derived from the often misused Hagalaz rune just as it can be from the Cabalistic scheme of things.

What species of tree we are talking about is almost if not completely unimportant. In European culture much has been made in recent times of the ash, though in my view this is based on a mistake. The ash ("*ask*' or '*ashk*') is a powerful aspect tree for the sedentary peasant farmer, as many tools and useful articles can be made from its wood. The 'golden fleece', however, along with the idea of ongoing faith even in the darkest night (as the 'red apples in winter'), are Kennings suggesting the yew. In Siberia it may well be the birch; in New Zealand no doubt it is the kauri, and in India of course the Bodhi tree or pipal.

If you ask the trees themselves, you will find the question which tree the World Tree is to be a matter of sublime indifference to them. As a grumpy old oak in a famous Irish valley observed, 'Everyone has to climb his own tree.'

The same wisdom has been preserved practically in pure form in the mysteries of the Elder Edda. The journey of humanity leads through the material World Tree, on which the human being, through his own attachment, practically sacrifices himself. This is beautifully expressed in the 'Hangatyr' or Hanged God Wuotan, who hangs himself on the World Tree and purges himself.

Only after acknowledging his errors, which ultimately led to the war between the Aesir and the Vanir and his subsequent rejection by Frigg, does he acquire a new form as the solitary wanderer 'Grimnir' and finally, through his passion on the World Tree, becomes able to let go, falls to the ground, learns the wisdom of the runes and the counsel of Mimir and Völva.

It is only by letting go of himself that he regains his own divinity, and so becomes capable of claiming his rightful place, which during his exile has been usurped by his cruel deputy 'Ullr/Loki', who rules not from the heart but based on cold justice and greed. Our true being cannot be replaced by an emotionless set of rules.

This passion of hanging on a tree – leading to the purification of the material and realisation of one's own divinity – is something also undergone by Jesus Christ on the cross, as well as by Gautama Buddha sitting under the Bodhi tree.

In the Vedas, the key to self-understanding is stated to be the diving down to the roots of one's own lotus on the floor of the cosmic ocean. Only in this way does the creator become conscious of the power of his own thoughts.

The Greek Argonauts led by the hero Jason, as the legend relates, managed to reach the World Tree and steal the golden fleece from it. A clue might be the ancient oak sanctuary in Dodona, where oracular powers were ascribed to the sounding copper cauldrons suspended in the branches of the trees or the rustling of leaves. The wisdom of the oracle was attributed to the 'Magi' of the land of 'Barbar'.

Christianity too has its world tree, both in the Cross and in Jacob's Ladder. From the highest angelic spheres to the darkest regions at the root, the World Tree, in more or less complex cosmic schemes, penetrates and extends through all levels of being.

Celtic cognitive models based on trees

To convene their understanding of the omnipresent natural laws, the Druids created models, dictae and songs. The particularly gifted bard Amyrgin for example encrypted the most important essential features of different trees in his ballad 'The Battle of Trees'.

A most important model is the Triskelia: Three primeval forces in movement on earth: air, water and fire. Along with the element of earth itself, that makes a total of four. This gives rise to the well-known Celtic cross, with the element of life or love as the central part connecting to all the others. All five elements can take on several different emphases and merge into one another in different ways. There are good grounds for comparing this with the five phases of transformation of the Chinese. The primeval source is the same in all cases.

In recognising the deep secrets of the fifth, binding force as love through which life is called into being the Culdaic Druid monks were not alone but foremost.

According to Celtic legend, Ogma Sun Face created his own Ogham alphabet on the principles of the Celtic cross and five concentric rings, as a basis not only for messages but also for the coding of various mnemonics. At some time not so very long ago, finally, a rather dabbling Neo-Druid tried to classify trees based on their different qualities mixed with zoroastric horoscopy and the ogham alphabets. The resulting circle of trees is very esoteric and that's it.

Nordic mysticism, finally, gives us further attributes and keywords, so called kennings for different trees, which have been handed down from primeval times. Indeed according to the Edda, the first two human beings, Ask and Embla, have been created by Odin, Thor and Loki from two pieces of driftwood.

How to find suitable trees

Take your time and enjoy the journey. The value of a pilgrimage lies in the fact that even while travelling you can leave behind the ballast of everyday thoughts, become inwardly calm and attune yourself to what is to come. Even if you arrive at a specific place by train, car or aeroplane, it makes sense to cover the last few kilometres on your own feet, just to get acquainted with the genius of the location. This may involve aimless meandering around in a wood, or else the deliberate approach to a specific tree. To begin with I would advise you to visit large, healthy specimens.

Try to relax while you are walking - just hang loose. Simply attune to all things you may encounter. This is known as multipointed walking meditation. Be as relaxed and openminded as you can. If thoughts of everyday intrude, just let them surface, and then gently but firmly put them aside, like you hang a worn coat on a nail, as you continue on your path. This needs a lot of practice. The bigger the worries of everyday, the longer you should decide to journey. In all religions, this is the deeper meaning of pilgrimage.

When you arrive at your tree, you will know it at once. It just radiates a magical attraction for you. Take a good look at it! Observe it with all your senses, your entire being. What does it look like? In what sort of surroundings is it situated? Does it have animals living in it? Do you sense a slight change in wind, or temperature? Do you feel anything else? Often trees greet travellers with a gentle rustling of their leaves.

To get a complete impression, you would be well advised to circle the tree thoughtfully three times, at a certain distance. Ideally anticlockwise, as that means that your left, feeling-focused side will be turned to the tree.

As soon as you sense something like a warm attraction, retaining your relaxed state, calmly move into the zone between the root ball and the crown.

Sacrifice, puja, ritual: the loving gesture counts

If you feel inclined, you are welcome to 'sacrifice' some small token to the tree. While you are walking on your way to the tree you will often find something you can offer. White pebbles, fallen blossoms or leaves, whatever takes your fancy. Water poured over the roots will do as well. To this day, there are regions of Brittany, Ireland, Wales, India, Russia and Japan where coloured ribbons or paper strips are attached to low-hanging branches of trees.[1]

You can work out your own ritual, making it as a complex as you like, with drink offerings, the recitation of hymns or verses, presentation of gifts or dancing; or simply send the tree your sympathetic feelings in thought. Anything that is not going to damage the tree, and testifies to your sympathy, is permitted. In the last resort it is your sympathetic feelings that allow you to connect with a tree. It should come from the heart, or not at all.

You should avoid things made of metal or plastic. Money, tobacco, alcohol or other drugs are unlikely to be well received.

Often gifts are associated with the request for help with more or less everyday problems. This may work on occasion but does not entitle the giver to any kind of claim in the sense of a Nordic sacrifice. In an ancient text we read the sacrifice should spring 'from the red blood of the heart'. This means the heartfelt sacrifice of 'red' love not associated with demands.

It once and for all doesn't mean a bloody sacrifice! The sacrifice of living beings, or of gifts created through suffering or destruction like blood, animal sacrifice and any incitement of others to such acts, is under geas[2] of the Lord of the Forests and banned once and for all under pain of more than lethal punishment. You don't want that. Trust me!

---

[1] Use natural materials in short strips, tying the strips loosely, so as not to present a hazard to animals and to avoid constricting the branch.
[2] A *geas* is a Celtic form of taboo. Violating it always results in drastic to inhuman punishment. To be effective it has to be in accord with the great balance. All disharmony in it backfires!!

As soon as you sense a certain warmth or sympathy, you can go up to the trunk and touch it with the palms of both hands.

Make sure you are standing in a good place, preferably not on the roots, and close your eyes. The calmer you have succeeded in becoming on your way to the tree and to presenting your gift, the more likely you are to perceive a peculiar oscillation, as if you were alternately expanding and contracting. Other phenomena may also occur. Don't be afraid if they do, they are nothing to worry about. It is just the tree taking your measure. What you are sensing is a kind of pulsing, which takes place in the trunk all the time. And if the tree should want to communicate something to you, it will do so in his own time and measure - one way or another.

Enjoy the contact as long as you like, and then take your hands off the tree. – Congratulations: you have just communicated successfully with a tree for the first time!

After that you can sit down under the tree and spend a bit of time there, or you can say goodbye at once.

The important thing in all this is that you should be relatively undisturbed yourself to be able to feel the presence of the tree without interference from inner or outer influences. This is one reason, incidentally, why children can very quickly succeed in getting in contact with a tree, if they wish to do so.

When no tree is within reach

'Mens sana in corpore sano'[3] – not just a homespun proverb of the Ancient Romans, the Chinese knew it as well: This was why they invented Kung Fu for hotheads, Tai Chi for more relaxed natures and Chi Gong for everybody. Two of their eight 'brocade exercises' were taken from trees. Consequently, they are actually called 'Embracing a tree' and 'Standing like a tree'.

If for whatever reason you have no access to a tree, I warmly recommend that you try the eight brocade exercises, and these two in particular. If you are lucky enough to have a LuJong (Tibetan healing Yoga) teacher around try it. Most of their exercises are based on soft movement of the spine – your innermost stem.

Embracing a virtual tree

Stand, or if not possible, sit upright, with your legs opened to the width of your shoulders, not quite fully extended. Distribute your weight in such a way that it rests as evenly as possible on the soles of your feet. Sink into your knees by about half a hand's breadth and bend the hips, to take the weight off the vertebral column. Stretch the crown of your head towards the sky while pulling in your chin, to take the strain off the cervical vertebrae. Now you are already standing with your vertebral column like a tree.

As is standard with such exercises, you should pay attention to your breath, breathing in through the nose and slowly and deeply out through the mouth. Once you have come to a state of rest, while breathing in you lift both hands in front of your chest, palms inward and slightly angled arms, the hands roughly at the level of the abdomen, the fingertips of both hands just an inch apart.

When breathing out you turn the palms downward and lower your arms. Carry on breathing and concentrate on the space between the opposed fingertips. Align the fingertips of the mutually opposed fingers to one another. Don't forget the thumbs!

---

[3] 'A healthy mind in a healthy body'.

As soon as you feel the energy in the fingertips, you can begin to play with it: when breathing in, you can slowly distance the hands from one another, and when breathing out, bring them together again. In this way, you are pumping the breath of life, mana, prana, lung, chi, or simply the life energy through your channels.

You can vitalise specific parts of the body with the field of life energy so created, by approaching these parts as you raise or lower your hands. Your hands are working in this exercise like a kind of parabolic mirror. The level of the energy you generate will be determined by the correct posture, breathing and hand position.

Standing like a tree
Stand upright. Lower your hands, with the palms turned inward, to the upper legs, and lift them a bit higher every time you breathe in. When breathing out you lower them a little bit.

Repeat this until you are like a bird, beating its wings in a leisurely way in harmony with the breath. Turn your Palms upward. Lift your arms higher and higher, until they touch above your head. Now leave them above your head, and this time feel the force which flows through the palms, which are now turned outward, right down into your feet. You are standing like a tree.

Now imagine that you are a tree with its branches in the wind, and its roots deep in the earth. Feel the wind, the rain and the sun, as they surround you and charge you with energy.

The better you will be able to visualise, the more intense your tree experience will be. In your imagination you can visualise any kind of tree you like: ash, coconut or mango, it's your choice.

To finish, just lower your arms sideways to your upper legs, and softly breathe out to come back to reality. This very powerful exercise is still practised today by shamans, mystics and Druids all over the world.

Talismans

The last, and one of the most effective ways of staying constantly in touch with a tree is with the help of a piece of wood of the same tree. With a properly shaped and activated piece of wood, you can bring the tree of your choice to mind at any time, and in rare cases even get into dialogue with it and use its strength.

The strength of the exchange will depend on the depth of your connection with the tree. But on no account should you injure a tree in getting your piece of wood. Suitable talismans, wands, wooden worry objects and a whole lot more, along with detailed instructions may be ordered from www.druidenwissen.ch. Just send me a mail.

Sick and injured trees

Sick trees communicate unhealthy thoughts and feelings. If a tree is evidently sick or injured, you should help it physically before you try to contact it. If it is just a small injury, a tree wound dressing will generally be found effective – you can get this in any good garden centre. If it is a fungal infestation, matters are more difficult. Here you need to resort to the assistance of a specialist. Sometimes even seriously injured trees can heal completely and go on to have a long and healthy life.

On and around particularly massive trees you will often find traces of our 'excessivilisation'[4]: rubbish of all kinds littering the ground and the bark. Rather than grumbling about it, I always carry a small plastic bag, with which most of such rubbish can soon be made to disappear.

Most trees are particularly nagged by metal objects in their bark or immediate vicinity, like thumbtacks or staples. Even if they are not lodged deeply in the wood, their magnetic fields still interfere with its perception of the tree's electromagnetic surroundings and feel like a splinter. With a small pair of pliers, you can carefully resolve the problem.

It is rarely any good trying to remove wires or broken nails and the like that have grown deep into the bark. The resulting damage to the tree would usually be worse than the original irritation. Some beeches and hornbeams have fence wire completely covered over by the bark, and it doesn't seem to bother them at all.

Right at the start of my dealings with trees, I met a beech which had suffered a small wound in the bark as a result of careless forestry operations. I got into contact with it and tried to encourage the wound to close by the power of imagination. I imagined I could take the tear from the tree and close it up in short order.

As our fireplace, situated on the hiking trail, was directly below, separated by a steep and stony slope, I tried to slide down it. The inevitable happened – I lost my balance and landed most ungracious flat on my belly in the mud, much to the amusement of my companions of course. As a result, I grazed my hand.

The resulting injury was just the same shape as the wound on the tree.

---

[4] Sic! – excessivilisation = excessive civilisation.

Spirit of the wood, individual dryad, nymph or deva
The trees of a wood stand close together. As a result, the signals from an individual tree are often lost in the general communicative field of the wood. The ancient Druids were in the habit of visiting the woods to ask for counsel, as the collective consciousness of many trees is extremely powerful. For this purpose, they even planted their own groves, known as 'Nemeta', to conduct their congregations there with guidance from the Spirit of the Wood. This was not to be done in a hurry, as several trees often need a very long time before they come to an agreement.

With tree groups consisting of the same species the problem is unlikely to occur, as the being of a tree, strange as this may sound, can constitute a collective consciousness in several representatives of the same species.

This collective being is known as a deva to the Indians. Devas are very different from one another, not just in their appearance but also in their being in relation to us. While the bright birch generally has the fresh appearance of a young girl, the oak is often hardened like an ancient warrior. All the same, in what concerns their being they are mostly comparable within their different families.[5]

And yet every tree is an independent individual in its own right. This shows clearly in the unique growth pattern. Depending on the environmental conditions, two trees of the same species can take on very different forms and characteristics.

---

[5] For example all the evergreen conifers, rosaceae, thuyas etc.

The time of day and season make a difference. What is a year for us is but a day, a day but a breath for them. Consequently, many trees have the habit of shedding their leaves in the late autumn and reducing their metabolism and go to sleep during the winter. Most trees rest during winter– except for some evergreens, like the yew, the fir and the holly.

Therefore, please don't bother them in winter unless it is really necessary, and don't be surprised if the tree fails to respond and continues its sleep. In the summer heat of noon, on the other hand, some deciduous trees are often too busy absorbing solar energy and photosynthesising to talk with us.

Proprietorial claims on a tree

Different people can communicate simultaneously with the same tree and may experience fundamentally different perceptions and impressions. In short, one tree holds room for many people. It will resonate with each person separately. However, it can also happen that the presence of one or more other people itself has an influence on the nature of our communication.

People may possess a tree in its physical form, of course, but not the indwelling life energy (chi, breath of life) or the divine soul spark which penetrates all life. It is not possible for a human being to own a deva.

If the Druids were denied access to a tree – or worse, if the tree had been maliciously killed – they did not fail, first of all, to curse the perpetrator from the bottom of their heart (or mug) and would then, as a next step, visit a less exposed specimen of the same species in order to communicate in secret with the same deva via a different physical tree.

How exactly to go about this will be described in the later section 'Help! - My tree has fallen.'

Things to avoid

For the sake of completeness, let me just mention here that it is absolutely never acceptable to damage a tree, that is to remove living parts of it by violence. Even pulling off leaves is bad manners. If a tree wants to give you something, it will generally be a dead branch, exuded resin or ripe fruits. Never take anything that has not been given!

And then there are those Druids who feel a compulsion to climb every tree in sight... For quite a lot of them, this ended in an abrupt and painful descent. Others got to a quite considerable height and wished for nothing so much as to be on the ground again but didn't know how to get down. Quite apart from this, the bark and bast fibre of most trees is very sensitive and will be crushed by hard shoe soles. Standing beneath its crown is perfectly sufficient.

Finally, there are those know-it-all shamans who first fog their consciousness with all kinds of drugs in order to have a 'supersensuous' experience. Drugs can open doors, but you never know what being is going to address you, and the price might be higher than any benefit you acquire.

Only the ignorant try to fly with drugs. Real Druids are proud of their waking consciousness, and sharpen it with attentiveness, observation and meditation. And no: I am not going to discuss this! Neither do the trees! A foggy mind can neither have clear thoughts nor clear emotions.

To meditate we need to be clear, calm and clean like a crystal in the sunlight. - But let us return to the main subject:

Nature's masterpieces

In environmental sciences, we learn the following facts: trees consist of the roots, the trunk and the crown. The roots are often strangely similar to the crown, only upside-down.

Trees are chemical factories, which produce biomass from water, carbon dioxide and certain substances from the earth, with the help of sunlight. Scientists are really excited about that process called photosynthesis, which represents a masterly cascade reaction for the biosynthesis of CO_2 into biomass.

Bionic scientists are fascinated by the tree's capacity to add mass just in the places where stability is needed, and even reduce it where it is not. Engineers are delighted to apply the same technique in mechanical engineering.

Pharmacists meanwhile are enchanted with the substances acquired from plants. Many synthetic medicines have their inspiration from plant substances.

System ecologists investigate the mutual interaction between living beings and their environment. This forms a basis for the derivation of useful models (the mosaic-cycle concept, strategic networks etc.) having relevance to economics, military strategy and other fields.

Every discipline contemplates and understands certain aspects of trees from their own angle.

But as far as I know, no scientist has ever yet asked the tree, as a living being, for its own point of view.

The holistic perspective

The elders of the Druids used to meditate in sacred groves and would ask the trees for counsel. They researched the mystery of the mutual interaction between entities on material, energetic and spiritual levels.

In order to preserve this knowledge and other aspects of wisdom, they created a powerful model, at a time even before the big migration: The World Tree. This model survived amongst others in Germanic, American Indian, Arabic and Russian mysticism.

It was the World Tree Yggdrasil on which Odin hung (being crucified at the same time) to accomplish his transformation from the hot-blooded warmongering 'Wuotan' to the wise far-seeing Odin. Hanging on the tree can also be seen as standing for the journey through all levels of the World Tree. Like a human being, every tree stands upright and has an 'above' and a 'below'. Between the crown and the roots, the trunk extends.

Roots

Let's start right at the bottom with the roots, in the earth kingdom of the dwarves, the elementals of earth and stone. This is where the tree has its 'rootedness', as the saying has it. It is only the root that makes it possible for a plant to grow irrespective of the location. To do this, it absorbs water, nitrogen, carbon, phosphorus and (depending on the plant) other substances as well, in a specific and appropriate ratio from the ground.

In storms, it is crucial, both for trees and for human beings, to have solid roots in order to remain standing. Therefore, for us humans as well, it is important, to wisely choose a place that suits us for the central focus of our lives, or else work persistently to make it habitable, penetrating hard ground with our roots.

Not every ground is suitable for anyone: Birches are able to populate barren tips of great height long before other trees, because they can take all the substances they need from the rubble. A beech makes different demands on the soil, and so will hardly be the first tree to appear on a scree slope.

Some if not most plants resort to assistance from their colleagues in the kingdom of the gnomes, the mycorrhizal fungi, in order to draw nutrients from the soil and gradually transform it.
On difficult terrain, we too would be well advised to learn from the tree's roots and surround ourselves with helpers who give us stability and security like roots do with the mycorrhizal fungi.

The quantity of all the plants at a given location often permits us to draw conclusions about the subsoil and the 'genius loci', the spirit of the place. On totally unsuitable ground, the dryad of a tree will move on, even if a seed is present. If an environment makes us ill, and cannot be transformed into fruitful soil by persistence, we can take an example from the trees and relocate to another environment at the earliest opportunity. The above can be considered for all our living, loving and working environments.

The mythology of the ancient Druids knows of three sources, and three main roots, which supply the Tree of Life with water and nutrients. Depending on the branch of the Druid tradition, the three mayor aspects of life have been called Parcae by the Greeks, Norns by the Vikings, amongst others. The wellbeing of the entire tree is always dependent on these three mysterious women.

For us human beings this means that in all three major walks of life, work, family and religious belief – or at least in one of these areas we have a need to put down strong roots to prosper in all three stages of life.[6]

---

[6] Word to the wise: Love is what unites them all.

Trunk

It's fascinating to contemplate a tree-disc: the heartwood at the core, then the sapwood conducting mineralized water upward, the cambium, the bast fibre layer conducting sweet sap downward to wherever it's needed and finally the protective bark on the outside. The ancient Druids were so impressed by this view that they used it as the basis for another cosmic model: At the innermost centre, the paradise of eternal peace. Around this, the form of the real world, and outside it everything else. It´s not just valid for trees: we human beings too have a divine core of our being, a real mode of appearance, and sometimes also a 'rough exterior'.

The ancients believed there are several such clearly defined disks like levels or worlds on the way from the root to the crown. Wandering between those worlds was for them, like the ascent of Jacob's Ladder, a way of travelling between various existing realities within the World Tree. Incidentally this is still the case today for the shamans of Siberia. Such a journey happens either when the shaman physically climbs a tree, or else when journeying in a state of trance.

A self-declared neo-shaman of my acquaintance explained the whole world succinctly, as it can be perceived by one person at one moment and on one level, as a disk like this with clear boundaries between the centre, the perceptible and the not personally perceptible world. If your own disk is free of tension and in balance, that which relates to it is likewise in equilibrium. This is subject to the ancient Druid saying, 'as above, so below; as without, so within'.

If certain regions of someone's trunk have got out of harmony, the Druids were acquainted, like Chinese medicine, to reharmonize them with the model of the pentagram in a circle, also known as the pentacle and consisting of five phases of transformation and their possible mutual relations. – Fascinating what can be apprehended just by studying a simple tree trunk, isn't it?

Crown

Every tree is royal: each wears its own crown from the point where its trunk divides into a number of branches, and finally lateral and terminal branches.

If we take a closer look at the structure from the point of view of the trunk, we can see that the external appearance of different trees is to a great extent defined by the structure and form of their crown.

Trees, like people, have several strategies for investing their life force. Firs mostly put everything into a strong main shoot. But if it breaks, it's a poor lookout for the fir.

Ash trees, and even the hazel, put their faith from the start in many different branches from the same root, which can be almost or entirely independent.

There are even some trees which deliberately lower their branches to the ground, in order to take root again with them.

Like this every tree shows its character and its strategy of thriving by the form of its crown. When studying different crowns, you will note all trees adapt perfectly to their environment. In a forest the same kind of tree will choose a different form than in open space. It's like our human life which may differ a lot from hermit to big city dweller.

Branches

With their branches, the trees give us an indication how to proceed: always towards the light!

Where in trees the main branches defining the form or main strategy in life, the small twigs, finally, are something like your daily tactical decisions in life. The right ratio of branching out, and the direction in which you extend your branches, are the important things here.

Different strategies of this kind are also found in the human world. If you pin all your hopes on a single branch – in career terms, in your family or your religious belief – you would be well advised to be elastic and enduring in this area, like a fir.

Someone, on the other hand, who has a lot of different branches or supports in one area does well to follow a tree's example, by remaining aware of equilibrium and the strain on the different branches at all times.

Managers would speak of the tactical or operational level. If a small twig breaks off or dries up, it may be tiresome, but it isn't the end of the world.

In this way human beings, like trees, can prevent tensions arising between different parts of their crowns.

Leaves

Leaves, every single one of them, are individual miracles of nature. With the help of the leaf pigment chlorophyll, the carbon of the carbon dioxide in the air is split by a certain wavelength of sunlight in a unique, organochemical cascade and processed along with nitrogen into a kind of sugar. This is carried by the hydrological circulation of the tree to the right points, where it is transformed and incorporated in the tree with the help of substances derived from the earth.

There are as many different leaves and needles as there are species of tree. It also depends on the location what kind of leaf strategy trees go in for. Each species has its own strategy for capturing sunlight and carbon dioxide. The trusting fir puts its faith in persistence. It has needles, so the snow isn't going to tear off branches or freeze its leaves.

The branches of the larch cannot sustain such a heavy load of snow as those of the elastic fir, which is why it sheds its needles in the autumn. If, like the holly, you stand in the heart of the wood, under the shady foliage of other trees, you are well advised to opt for exceptionally efficient leaves, so you can benefit from the last remnants of sunlight and hang onto your frost-proof leaves even in winter when other trees lose theirs. This is known as an acyclical niche strategy, in synecology and marketing alike.

Trees are real sun-worshippers. With their arms raised to the heavens and their feet anchored deep in the earth, they transform every ray of sun into pure life energy. The analogies asking to be drawn, with fruit, pollination and the role of symbiotic insects and pests, could easily fill a whole book.

Just one thing to mention at this point: trees are generous hosts, and love all kinds of animals and human beings, provided they stick by the tree's rules. Someone who ignorantly eats of the yew may be punished lethally in the same way as one who incautiously climbs on an alder buckthorn.

The timescale of trees

The tree's sense of time is different from that of human beings. Seen from our point of view they are never in a hurry but do everything in a leisurely way and with dignity.

One human solar day corresponds to a single breaths time in the plant kingdom. During the course of a day a tree takes one deep breath in, absorbing CO_2 and releasing O_2 (oxygen) into the air and every night it deeply breathes out once.

What is a year for us, is no more than a day in the tree's timescale. In spring they wake up, in summer they are fully awake and productive, in autumn they see the fruits of their day's work and in winter most of them sleep. Depending on the kind of tree they sleep more or less deeply then. Therefore, in winter it is better to seek out other trees that are not sleeping.

Deciduous trees go into deep sleep and shed their leaves, so they won't have to put up with a heavy load of snow and pressure from the wind. Conifers put their growth on hold but stay half-dozing.

Only the holly tree celebrates the winter with leaves and berries being itself a symbol of 'bending under the cold load without breaking', staying awake.

The trees field of resonance

Have you ever just felt really good or bad in the presence of a person, without touching them? Sometimes it is enough just to think of someone or something, and your whole feelings and emotions change instantly. Then you have felt their charisma, or what New Age esoterics call the 'aura'. It feels like a relative magnetic field between you and the other entity.

The seers among the Druids received their visions through resonance. By mastering these energies, the bards were able to heal or harm people with words and melodies trough resonance.

Trees, in this sense, are like Druids. They heal and harmonize through exercising an influence on our energy structures. To do this they make use of their own energy field, which is situated between the root ball and their crowns canopy like between the poles of a rod magnet.

In scientific terms, this is easy to explain by the potential difference between glucose-saturated descending sap and rising unsaturated sap in the tree. The magnetic part can be measured but the field of a tree consists of much more than just an electric field. I am sure New Age people have photographed the aura of trees. This should yield nice pictures of it.

When we approach its force field, the tree becomes able to perceive us directly as well. When we enter the inner zone between the root ball and the crown, we enter its house.

The experience we then have will depend very largely on our own internal world, as well as on the tree we have chosen because it is a relative interaction between you and the tree. Lots of people, especially when sleeping or meditating under trees, have found thoughts of various spiritual tree beings surfacing in their minds.

Getting into a meditative state
If you are already good at meditating, just sit down under a tree and meditate until you reach inner calmness. If things then surface in your mind that do not originate from your ego, congratulations: very probably the tree or one of its 'inhabitants' has just had an influence on you.

But if, like me at the start of my Druid training, you have not the slightest clue about meditation or inner calmness, just practise the following method as often as you can. Then sooner or later you will become able to feel the gentle wise whispering of the trees.

Chakras
In the most ancient roots of Druid teachings, we find indications that they used different intellectual models. In order to connect with other living beings on the energetic level, we need one that was created in ancient India.[7] It is the Vedic chakra or energy centres model.

According to this model every living being has a certain number of different chakras. Plants, animals, bacilli and human beings as well. Each chakra has its own characteristic colour, sound, vowel etc.

If you sense or resonate with the resulting energy field that emanate from the chakras of another entity, you are in resonating contact with it. This also can happen through pure imagination and imaginative resonance. It is also possible to consciously resonate just with certain chakras of a being, as when we are in love.

Let's first take a look at the different chakras of the human being. We will then go on to consider the chakras and energy fields of trees.

---

[7] Probably before the migration of peoples around ca(!) 3500 B.C. which led to the Persian Magi's splitting off from the European Druids.

The human chakras

At the moment of fertilisation, the human genome organises itself in the form of a spindle along an acid-base gradient within the ovum. In its distribution, this gradient corresponds to the wavelengths of a rainbow.

Only when this 'wedding' of the two genomes has been successful along the rainbow does new life come into being. This personal 'rainbow' will accompany each human being for the length of his or her life. It is not something fixed, however, but changes in the course of early childhood, puberty, adolescence and old age.

Along with what the person has inherited, over time increasingly their own experiences and deeds become part of their personal rainbow.

The Hindi and Buddhists speak of different kinds of 'karma', as the totality of all influences on the chakra framework of a human being.

But how can we imagine these chakras, or colours of our own rainbow? It's easy – just fill up a bath tub, and then pull out the plug! The eddy that forms looks just like a revolving chakra.

It has a clearly defined front, where the water is sucked down, and a back, where water flows down the drain in the form of a spiral.

The transmitting part of our chakras faces the front, the receiving part the back. Roughly speaking, the chakras give off light to the front and darkness to the back.

The ancient Druids knew that three master chakras reside in every humans 'House of the three suns', having the colours red, yellow and blue. They compared them to the elemental triskelia consisting of fire, earth and wind. These primary colours are then linked and extended by three more 'fire wheels' in orange, green and violet as the uppermost colour. This makes a complete rainbow.

The inner smile

As Martin Luther once said, 'A sorry arse never yet let a cheerful fart.' Therefore, it is important, before meditating, first to release all physical tensions and any pains you may have, as far as possible. The predecessors of the Druids understood the connection between body, soul and spirit. They taught simple physical exercises which, when regularly practised, alleviate many tensions and problems without the need of medicine, and may actually succeed in healing them completely.

In our own day these traditions are found in various forms of yoga, various physical exercises in the eastern and western traditions like the Tibetan breath techniques or the salutation to the Sun, and above all in LuJong, Kung Fu, Tai Chi and Chi Gong.

For our purposes, a bit of vertebral circling will do the trick. If you have mastered one of these relaxation techniques, you can use it before meditating instead of the one described below. If you are already quite loose and relaxed, you can even start to meditate directly.

The inner smile

In order to get in contact with other living beings on the spiritual level, we have to open our inner world, our innermost disk to influences of other beings. To do this, we only need to attune our chakras to a receptive state, so to speak.

The meditation of the inner smile opens our senses for the communication with trees. It is not the only one possible for this purpose. But it has proved, to be highly effective, as well as beneficial to health. Moreover, it is not tied to any religion or religious belief. Although its origins are lost in the mists of the pre-Celtic period, it has been extended by the latest insights up to the present day, being passed on in this form, while retaining its essential core.

Limits of the method

It is very important to set aside your own thinking patterns and expectations. What comes into your mind generally consists of feelings, patterns, pictures and occasionally even whole sentences. In principle this kind of meditation can also be practised with other living beings, like animals and people, standing stones, creeks rivers and so on. The results will differ widely because they have a different kind of waking consciousness or unconscious frequency.

Please note: what you see in the meditation will probably have little or nothing at all to do with the free will of the animal or person you meditate upon. Unless, of course, the communication on both sides has been of a deliberate kind. Cats are sometimes very good at this, but never climb into the lion's cage after meditating with its spirit. The lion itself would probably consider you as lunch!

Every beginning is easy

To begin with, you will undoubtedly need more than half an hour for the exercise described here, which is a preparation for actual tree communication. Nevertheless, don't worry. I took a whole lot longer at the start. Nowadays I only need some seconds. Practice makes the master, and right from your very first meditation, the time you spend on it will definitely prove rewarding.

Releasing tensions

Stand with your feet apart, at shoulder width. Your pelvis should be tilted forward, the knees slightly bent. Your hands rest lightly, with open fingers and the palms down, on your back at the level of the kidneys. The hands should not exercise any pressure on the back. Like this your whole spine is completely straight.

You now shift your weight gently onto your right leg. This results in a shift of the load on your feet. Your hip and abdomen now shift to the right, until you meet with resistance. Here you should notice a slight shifting of the weight on your feet as well, perceptible on the right side of the foot. Only go as far as the point where you sense resistance.

You then shift your weight and your hip, moving very slowly in a circle, towards the back; then to the left, and finally to the front. You should repeat this circle at least nine times. While doing this, your head should always remain at about the same height and in the same spot. Don't arch your back. The load on the soles of your feet should always be clearly perceptible to the maximum in the direction to which the hip is inclined.

The entire circling movement should be carried out as slowly as possible and without any effort. Clicking and the release of joints and the vertebrae are normal but should never be forced.

If you feel pain, do not forcibly press into it, but go slightly less far, so that the pain does not occur. Your hands should be gently supporting your back throughout the exercise, so that the back doesn't cave in.

After several slow turnings of the hip, you can involve the chest region in the circling movement as well. You now turn the hip region much less, but focus principally on the upper body, in a continuation of the same circling movement. Here, of course, your head is no longer going to stay put. Again: the important thing is still not to force it, and above all, circle slowly.

To finish, the shoulder region and the neck circle as well. The hands can now hang loosely alongside the body. Attention: the neck is very sensitive. When turning your head, don't bend your neck backwards but straighten it.

When your entire vertebral column has been loosened up in a clockwise direction, at some point you slowly bring the circling movement to a close, and then start from the head with the anticlockwise movement, carrying out the same exercise from the top down: neck, shoulders, chest, abdomen and finally the hip and knees.

Any tensions in your internal organs will also be brilliantly loosened up through this exercise. Don't worry about any burps or wind. True to the quotation we started with – just let it fly!

Waking up your own energy
Let us move on to the actual meditation, which opens the chakras and senses to such an extent that we will be able to communicate with trees.

Using the protective circle
When you meditate with a tree, you are in its sacred space between the root ball and the crown. If the tree is healthy, this space protects all the living beings within it very effectively against negative influences. But perhaps you may want to meditate in a different place and need to protect yourself against mental influences from without. To do this, trace a circle around yourself in the air with a stick, or just with your finger. Within this protective circle you can place five twigs, stones or whatever you like to form a pentagram. The arrangement of the elements on the five-pointed star corresponds with the phases of transformation (fire, air, water, earth, life), starting from the south.

It does not have to be the druidic pentacle: if you follow a system of belief, you can perfectly well lay a faith symbol of your own, like a cross for example. The four archangels will in this case protect the four points of the compass. However, the four directions of the cross can equally well represent fire and water and wind and earth.
At the centre you then have the element of life – love actually.

Meditate

Sit in the centre of your protective circle, with your back as straight as possible. Slightly incline your pelvis to the front. Slightly draw in your chin, so that the vertebral column is straight.

It isn't always easy to sit up straight when you are under a tree. Personally, I like sitting with my legs tucked up under me or in the lotus position. Generally speaking, this meditation can be practised in almost any position, even lying down or sitting on a branch. You can even sit admirably straight when perched on the edge of a stool.

It is important, that you should always be comfortable and your feet and legs shouldn't go to sleep or hurt. If they do, you can change your position at any time.

You should take care to be in a nice and quiet place, without any disturbance impinging on your eyes, ears, nose or taste, affecting your consciousness. This is why Druids, before meditating, often calmly take a sip of pure water and prefer it over any other drink.

Now spend a few breaths concentrating on your pulse. Take it easy and try to become inwardly calm. Empty yourself of thoughts in the following way: whenever a disruptive thought appears, imagine yourself grabbing it by the collar and putting it aside.

With some annoying thoughts you have to do this several times, before they eventually stay out of the way. Alternatively, you can concentrate on just one thought or object, for example a leaf, a twig or a crystal to become focussed. The ancients called this 'one-pointed meditation'.

Grounding

Once you are calm and focussed enough, imagine yourself in a protective shell. Picture yourself as being in an egg and surrounded with white light. This is a purely mental construct, but it is a wonderful help for keeping disruptive thoughts at a distance. Some Druids step by step expand this egg infinitely large and enclose everything within it in their love. But to start with I would suggest that about half a metre around you is an appropriate distance.

Now let your breathing become slower. For about five pulse beats breathe in deeply through the nose, first with the abdomen and only then by lifting your chest. Wait for two pulse beats before breathing out through the mouth, by evenly lowering the abdomen and chest, for the duration of about ten pulse beats.

When breathing in, you focus your consciousness on filling your entire body with energy. As you breathe out, you imagine yourself growing deep roots in the earth, starting from your tailbone and the soles of your feet.

Once you have got this working, every time you breathe in, you contract your perineal muscles[8] slightly and relax them again as you breathe out. This powerfully stimulates the energy flow along the spinal column.

As you continue breathing in this way, feel the energy mounting behind the sacrum with every inhale.

If you are still sitting straight, breathing calmly and deeply with your entire body, well-grounded through your roots and open your mind to the heavens, you have done enough for the first time and can terminate the exercise.

Practise this a few times before going on to the next step.

---

[8] The perineum is the lowest part of the torso, between the sexual organs and the sphincter.

Awakening the energy

When the exercise so far has become familiar to you, while breathing in imagine the energy of the sun or the stars flowing into you from above.

Concentrate in a relaxed way on the abdominal region around the navel. Asian wisdom calls this reservoir the lower dan-dien, the seat of the kundalini energy or hara.

Let additional breath energy flow from this region into the base chakra. Situated at the perineum, this is the seat of the lowest, the base chakra. Its colour is red, and it has a great deal to do with grounding, self-confidence and sexuality as well. The Druids refer to it as the lower sun. As you breathe out, you press the accumulated energy upward within the spinal column by tensing the perineal muscles. It will take a bit of practice before you can really feel the energy rising upwards along your spine like warm water.

Building the inner circle and harmonizing the chakras

Once your energy is rising up to the level of the kidneys, let it flow forward again through the body, and smile! You are cleansing both your base and your kidneys chakra. The colour of the kidney's chakra is orange. It has a great deal to do with life energy and trust in life, happiness and sadness.

This energy circulation to the front and down, through the red base chakra at the perineum, to the coccyx, to the back and up, is the foundation for feeling secure in yourself, and for opening all the other chakras. As soon as they are opened, they provide a channel for spiritual beings to contact us – provided both sides wish it.

Once you have got this mini-circulation through the kidneys and base chakra going smoothly, use your imagination to branch out with about half of the energy, sending it further up the vertebral column to the height of the solar plexus.

Let this energy too flow forwards through the solar plexus, to the front and down, again circulating into the perineum.

You will have guessed that we have now reached the third, the solar plexus chakra. Its colour is a golden yellow. It is responsible for our ability to process experiences like the belly processing food. Now you have activated three chakras already.

If this is all working nicely, let another part of the energy rise to the level of the heart and lungs, then flow out to the front through the lung chakra. The colour of the lung chakra, curiously, is green. However, for a Druid it is logical enough.

We breathe with our lungs, as trees breathe with their leaves. Leaves are green, so the lung chakra is green as well. It stands for breathing and processes of exchange with the environment. Just breathe out all the trash and become calm.

When this too is up and running, you can again let part of the energy rise to the height of the neck, supplying energy to this region as well. The colour of the throat chakra is a pleasing light blue.

This is responsible for our ability to communicate with the environment. Clean and harmonize all the chakras liberally with energy throughput, Congratulations: you are just harmonizing your whole system.

This is but a very basic description of the chakras but should be sufficient for the next step. The heart has not been left out. It will be cleansed separately. In this model the energies of the heart chakra would be all chakras together, a rainbow combined to pure white light.

Cleansing the house of the upper sun

As soon as you have mastered the art of cleansing the main chakras, you can follow on from the preceding meditation to bring the whole flow of energy up the spinal column and right into the head. Let the energy well up into your entire head like a fountain. Imagine it bubbling up and spreading out into your mind.

Now it can happen that you are not filled just with positive energy, or your energy reserves are a bit low. That's not a problem: just follow the tree's example, open the roof of your skull in thought, and let healing light from all the heavens above directly pour into you. You can imagine this heavenly energy as a pristine beneficial waterfall of clear, bright light from the heavens above.

Now open your foreheads chakra, situated between the eyes at the level of the base of the nose as well. Its colour is a very light violet, just on the verge of radiant ultraviolet. Its function is closely linked to true realisation and seeing. You can take in life energy through this chakra as well, by deliberately contemplating something beautiful or uplifting like an object of meditation, a candle, a beautiful view or whatever inspires you.

The ancient Druids used to let the golden sun shine directly on their brow. But be careful not to gaze into the sun with the naked eye! It's better to close your eyes. It's enough if your third eye replenishes its solar energy, that will cause your body to produce the happiness hormone.

Before you move on to the next step, imagine yourself getting the three mingled energies, your own, from heaven above, and from your third eye in front to whirl around in a circle in your head, like a circling galaxy, and so blending them thoroughly. To support the mingling of the heavenly sun with your own energy you can try to follow this whirl around with your eyes as well.

Now you should feel full of energy and at a deep inner peace.

The inward smile

If you're not already smiling, do so now. Just let your whole face relax. Feel the sun and the heavens above you, and your deep roots below.

Feel the life sap rising along your spine and being charged with solar power and heavenly energy at the highest point of your skull, the crown chakra.

Now it is time to let this whole positive energy flow into you. Continue to pay attention to your upright posture and your breathing. Let your tongue rest lightly on the roof of your mouth and be aware of any pleasant sounds: the twittering of birds, soft music or just the peace and quiet.

If you have closed your eyes, open them again and calmly look at something you find pleasant, whether it is a tree, people or a panorama.

As a third step, as you breathe in you absorb the pleasant scents or the pure air. This can be anything from the scent of flowers to the aroma of fresh coffee or incense. And last of all, you pay attention to the pleasant taste inside your mouth and become conscious of your tongue resting lightly on the palate.

Let the memory of these pleasant impressions register with you. They will protect you against any negative sensuous impressions in the further course of the meditation. The strength of the protection depends on your imprinting these sensations on your consciousness and is just a matter of practice.

Clean and harmonize all your senses: hearing, seeing, taste smell and touch. It is not important if there are sensual disturbances around at the moment, but to bring your senses in a peaceful state.

Purifying the emotions

Let's move on to the main part of the 'meditation of the smiling tree'. As you now have deep roots and an energy-charged tree crown, you can fill yourself with energy just as trees do all day long.

To do this, smile in a relaxed way and let the mingled energies of the heavens, the sun and your own energy flow like a warm current over your head, through the throat and down to around the level of your collar bones.

This is where your thymus gland is situated. Its function is that of a gatekeeper to the main body. It controls what things and emotions are allowed to get into and out of you. Fill it with the shining light energy flowing down from your mind, until it radiates a bright white light.

Let the energy flow further down, flowing into your lungs and filling them, until they have the clear shining blue of a bright morning sky, a blue of candour and honesty. It is the lungs that connect us with the element of air. They are responsible for what we exchange with our environment. – Honesty and outspokenness.

Carry on further, down to the heart. Fill it with love, until love makes it glow red. The heart not only pumps life through our veins, it is also the seat of love, in relation to oneself and other persons. Its element is fire. – It transforms and gives energy.

Continue downward and to the right to reach the liver. Fill it with energy and cleanse it until it shines with a bright rich grass green, full of sweet temper. The liver is responsible for detoxification and blood production. Its element is wood. – It cleanses our blood.

Then move to the left, to the spleen and the pancreas. Fill these with light energy, until they shine with the golden yellow of perfect understanding. The job of the spleen and the pancreas is to distinguish correctly and evaluate different kinds of nourishment, as well as other influences. Their element is the earth. – It nourishes us.

Last of all you let the energy flow down into your kidneys and fill them up, until they shine with a deep ocean blue, the colour of trust and faith in life. The job of the kidneys is to secrete and let go. Their element is water.

Let the energy flow back up again through the coccyx, now forming the big circuit, energy pulling up at the back cleansing and healing the chakras, adding and transforming through heavenly and solar energies at the top, flowing down at the front through the organs cleaning and healing them.

Linking circuits

Continue focusing on your breathing, deep down into the abdomen, the flow of incoming heavenly energy when you breathe in and the energy circuit, going up the spinal column, through the head to the front and down through the organs washing, cleaning and harmonizing them.

When you breathe out, contract the perineal muscles slightly and pump life energy upwards through the vertebral column, letting it fill your head as described above.

You should now be calm, focused and to some extent free from disruptive thoughts. If you are sitting with your back to a tree, extend your bodily shell in thought, letting the rising circuit go backwards and upwards. In this way you are making it possible for the tree, with its energy field, to come into contact and resonate with your force field, your chakras and your circulating energy.
Wait and pay attention to any kinds of thoughts that come up to the surface of your consciousness, like air bubbles in water – these may be in the form of colours, emotions or mental pictures.

Often tree beings signal their presence by a slight breeze. As soon as pictures or thoughts start to form in your mind, check to see whether these are just irritating thoughts of everyday, or input coming from outside yourself. Again: the tree may communicate with you in the form of feelings, fragmentary thoughts or fully formulated sentences. Just as with the thoughts in you, so you can deliberately form thoughts, for example, to ask a question. The answers will then come back in the same form, generally as words or images which tentatively form in your mind. Please note that trees can only communicate with you through the emotions, pictures or words that are in some sense present within you already.

Set aside any disruptive thoughts, lovingly but with decision.

Becoming aware

I admit first this meditation may seem difficult. Generating a steady flow of energy, steering it to the right places while being aware of posture and breathing does need some practice. The druids had to learn it step by step as well. Practise with patience and your efforts will be rewarded. Simply do the best you can. Just cleansing your chakras, senses and internal organs, even for the very first time, has a liberating and vitalising effect.

It is possible that you manage to make contact with a tree for the first time even before you have mastered this exercise. If you approach a powerful tree quite openly and give it your trust and your sympathy, you are sure to sense something. But in order to get in touch with a tree consciously, you should have understood this and the previous section to a certain extent. It doesn't depend just on the will to get into an exchange of ideas with a tree.

It is about the mental images already inside of you, through which the tree is able to make an impression on you. Therefore of course, as an Arab Sufi noted very perplexed, to an Arab a Swiss tree will talk Arabic. Even on a remote planet in a Galaxy far far away, all nonverbal communication[9] would be in your mothers' tongue.

It's as if you are wanting to paint a picture and the tree acts like a muse. Depending on the colours you have available, the picture may look quite different.

For those of you who are musically gifted, we could say that how a tune sounds is going to depend on the instrument. As the French observe: 'C'est le ton qui fait la musique.'

---

[9] Caveat: The cognitive conscious mind of your nonverbal communications partner may be influenced by you as well but, if it is a sentient being it will have its own, completely different cognitions than what it may have evoked in your imaginative resonance! Therefore, do not try to pet the tiger! Respect the other being's consciousness.

Beginning and maintaining communication

If you have carried out the preceding meditation, opened yourself in a state of peaceful calmness, and are in possession of a relatively intact knowledge about trees and their mode of consciousness, then you can begin to learn from their practically infinite wisdom and love.

To have faith in life's ever winding ways, comfort and knowledge and confidence in yourself and the future. And yes: finally, you may feel quite a bit of real magic, the essence of unconditional love.

When you talk to a tree, you should be polite. The deva you are talking to is lovingly disposed to you. Sometimes it may be another tree-being, resonating and inspiring your mind.

At the beginning, if unclear, simply ask who it is you are talking with, whether you are engaged in dialogue with the individual tree, which happens rarely, the deva of the genus, which is almost always the case, or even with the Lord of the Woods, or some charming fellow pretending to be one of them...

Presenting demands or wishes is usually pointless. Trees don't give a hoot for vain striving for power, glory, money, might or revenge. It is much the same with gossip and tittle-tattle of all kinds!

But if you ask questions about your personal path or important decisions, or about how to deal with a difficult situation, you will undoubtedly receive inspiration. Perhaps not an answer that is clear right from the start, but in the end the counsel of the trees will prove to be wise advice.

Do never expect orders or instructions but ideas and feelings. Trees will never ever advise you to harm any being. It simply is not in their nature.

If thoughts of violence should emerge in your consciousness, your mind is not in a calm meditative state. Remember: the thoughts that come into your mind will be limited by the pictures, words, thoughts and emotions in you that are already present and accessible in some form at that moment.

You may experience spirits of all forms: angels, devas, goblins, gnomes, totems, nature and animal spirits and even wise elders. Your perceptions may extend from ideas to sounds, even scents and sensations.
Or you may fall into a simple and healing drowsiness, a state of lucid dreaming. Your talk may be very brief, or it can go on for hours; it may be of a depth you have never imagined before. Leave yourself time and trust in the tree. Within the tree's protective circle, you are sheltered and secure.[10]

How and which contents the tree can communicate to you will be limited practically, only by the fund of mental images and feelings already present in you.

Therefore, the same tree may communicate in a completely different way with different people even at the same time. Perhaps you may make contact through the tree with a being who is important to you personally, while someone else will get a glimpse of a completely different being.

---

[10] But at all means do mind weather, seasons and "visitors". Ants and certain gnats can be as much a nuisance as obnoxious passerbys. – Reality is real: remember?

Ending communication

When you have learned what you want to know, or when the tree gradually brings the communication to an end, draw your inner circuit back into your body again, take a few deep breaths and open your awareness gradually to the everyday again.

Stay for a while and calmly convey your gratitude to the tree. If you feel like leaving a sign of your gratitude, then traditionally white, or occasionally coloured ribbons made of natural materials are the token of choice. Make sure they are loosely attached, so they aren't going to cut into the bark of the tree at a later stage, and so they won't alarm or harm animals.

Coins, tobacco and alcohol are not of the trees' world, and will prove toxic to the tree sooner or later. On the other hand, pebbles you have picked up on your way to the tree (especially white ones) are ideal. Then simply say bye and take your leave.

Of trees and children

It is said that there have even been big Druid trees that would only communicate through children. Children often are born professionals, when it is a matter of talking to trees.

Trees particularly hazel, will frequently speak to them without any kind of meditative preparation, as children's imagination is generally open, and they do not actively suppress new ideas from their consciousness. They are still nearer to the allfather and allmother than we grownups.

Children have their own kind of beautiful magic of imagination, clairvoyance and fantasy. – Sometimes this beauty is quite hard to detect. Just let them be beautiful as each child is.

At the same time children, with their uninhibited fantasy, and imagination tend to exaggerate now and then. And please don't force a child to talk to a tree.

Simply meditating in peace
Being pestered when meditating, is a real pain in the rear!
To prevent such interruptions, it makes sense to meditate in peaceful locations where you will have no nags hanging around. It does no good to put the blame on your phone, the children or anyone else. This is the reason why all cultures have built monasteries and cloisters as places of quiet meditation and peaceful tranquillity.

As but a few readers are likely to have a cloister at their disposal you could give it a start by trying to find quiet places with single trees or in the woods when you want to meditate. Churches are not bad either, but they happen to have few living things or even trees inside.

If you are meditating at home try to meditate during silent hours, switch off the phone and tell the other people in the house that you don't want to be disturbed.

Notwithstanding, some of the most beautiful village linden trees are situated in heavily populated areas. Moreover, even at the most secluded places you may find an ant or more dangerous a tick climbing up your trouser leg, which is going to have a serious effect on your meditative mood.[11]

Over the centuries several cultures have developed various methods for dealing with disturbances so that we won't have to miss the opportunity of talking to a village linden or give up meditating in noisy surroundings. It is not a matter of shutting oneself off in a kind of emotional cage but rather of resolving unpleasant situations in a spirit of respect and empathy.

---

[11] Always funny to contemplate very selfimportant druids bolting up and perform a merry hoparound after having unheedingly settled on an ant's highway. – Always check the spirit of the location before doing something. Not all gnats are harmless.

Indeed, meditation is possible in midst a city, even within its rumbling, vibrating soundscape. The only important thing is that no individual noises should stand out and attract your attention. Parks are the most suitable places, preferably ones with quiet visitors.

Some of the most beautiful trees are to be found in botanic gardens in midst the heart of cities. If you still feel disturbed by ambulance sirens, fire engines, crying babies and the like, you can try the following methods. The chances are that you'll be helping others besides yourself.

The stoic or Buddhist way is just to wait patiently until the unpleasant state comes to an end like all things eventually will. This is ideal for dealing with groups of hikers going past or barking dogs.

If you can do away with the cause of the interruption with a friendly word or by briefly lending assistance, so much the better.
Reacting with aggression or authority is usually pointless, as that will make your meditative mood vanish entirely. By the time you succeed in calming yourself down, the interruption would probably have gone by in any case.

The second more powerful (and magic) way is to picture the cause of the interruption, or the troublemaker, in your mind's eye as being in a situation of perfect harmony. You can also imagine the state of inter-ruption disappearing, until it actually happens. This silent and patient benediction takes some practice and time but can occasionally result in amazingly beautiful experiences.

Depending on your imagination and power of faith you can silently benedict almost any being in any situation. Just do it inconspicuously else the effect could be nullified. Do not even think of it as an instant solution. Sometimes it takes years to resolve a situation in those energies of loving light. If you think it takes longer to resolve the situation by power of loving imagination, then come back, when there will be no naggers hanging around or go elsewhere to meditate.

For instance, some years ago I was trying to meditate in the shade of a magnificent village linden. A bum with a bottle of beer in his hand was sitting just opposite me, staring fixedly in my direction.

I felt disturbed and decided to imagine this person as a happy and fulfilled human being in the heart of his family. Admittedly this does sound very odd, but after about half an hour the drunk was in fact joined by a young woman with shopping bags and two children. He put his bottle down on the bench and helped his wife to carry the shopping. Evidently, he had just been waiting till his family had finished their errands. After they had gone, I realised that it hadn't been beer, but a small bottle of apple juice, very similar in appearance, that he had been drinking. - I had just been given a free lesson on matters to do with prejudice. The linden above me murmured with its leaves in a satisfied way...

If the disturbance is impossible to ignore, and you can't just wait for it to pass, nor can you resolve the situation through love – when it is quite unbearable, in other words, just interrupt your meditation. It wasn't the right time. That sounds hard, but that's the way it is.

I had just started meditating with an ancient tree in a park, when the park attendant asked me to leave, as the park was about to be closed for the night. The above methods would hardly have been any good in this situation. Much to my regret I had to leave, but I came back the next day in a better mood and had several magnificent dialogues. When disturbances occur, there's always a reason for it. Listen quietly within. Perhaps there's another tree wanting to say something to you, and you will find it in a moment, only because you were just interrupted.

This is the way of dealing with disturbances the ancient Druids preferred. Every disturbance is perceived as being part of the cosmic fabric and but a short thread of your personal perceived reality. Therefore, every perception has its sense, including interruptions.

Sometimes it just isn't the right time

As in all life situations, there are suitable times and less suitable times for talking to trees. Try to talk to trees in pleasant weather during the growing season from spring to late autumn because in winter most trees tend to sleep. Besides you can easily catch a chill if you spend hours crouched beneath or sitting on branches in winter or freezing rain.

If during the cold season when all is barren and grey, you long for a sensible and caring counterpart, don't forget your Vitamin D and head for trees that do not shed their leaves in winter. All conifers, except the larch may be a bit sleepy but at least half awake in their trunk. Just the holly is fully awake and unyielding, gifting its berries to its friends when they need them most.

Concerning the weather, it is definitely not sensible to linger under trees in severe weather because you may either get a falling branch on your head, be literally enlightened when hit by a thunderbolt or if sitting in a tree lose your grip and find yourself heading to the ground in a most ungracious and hazardous way.

Please note that during the hottest time of the day or at midnight again there are very few trees likely to have something to say to you because they have fully inhaled or exhaled and our human system is most awake during the morning or in the afternoon.

At unsuitable times you best use your imagination, as described before. As strange as it may sound: the imagination of a blossoming tree in summer can give you the faint echo of a dialogue even in the depths of winter. It is entirely dependent on the power of your imagination and a matter of visualisation. It isn't much, but all the same it's better than getting a branch on your skull or catching a cold.

Sometimes highly advanced druids were able to have real contact with tree beings they knew very well even in the darkest dungeons.

Help, my tree has fallen!

If a tree has been blown down by a gale or felled by human hand, it's a fearful time not just for those who love trees but also for the dryads inhabiting it and the deva of the tree itself. When a tree dies, its individual consciousness, the dryad has several options. Most commonly it lingers for some time in the dying organism of the tree which is her home, and then takes refuge in a tree of the same species, melting into its consciousness. This is like two drops of water flowing together.

Sometimes when a very special tree has been felled thoughtlessly its dryad goes hunting for the perpetrator or whoever it takes for it, claiming his luck or life. You can appease and comfort the infuriated dryad by simply leaving a small token of your solace on the trunk.

The deva itself, as lord of the entire species, will carefully detach its consciousness from the tree, and is not weakened by the loss of one single individual tree as long as there are still enough other trees of the same kind. If the tree happens to be an exceptionally notable aspect tree or guardian tree of the wood, in the short or long term one or more other trees will take over its function.

You can help the dryad in a significant way and protect her from being unnecessarily decimated, by getting in touch with her before the fall of the tree if possible and showing her in your mind's eye the exact geographic path to a suitable tree of the same species. In your visualisation of this voyage make use of important waypoints like stones, mountains, lakes or any other landmarks.

This applies equally in the very rare situation where you really have to fell a tree. Explain to the dryad why you are obliged to take this step. If you like, you can also try to save several offshoots of the tree, in which you can invite the dryad to take up residence, when it is grown and has become strong enough. Maybe a part of her will then settle there.

My tree won't talk to me – what can I do?
Sometimes just when you think you really need its wise counsel a tree will remain silent. There's no point in goaching about it if you're not in a receptive state yourself, or if the tree just isn't in the mood. The fact is there are days where, like in human relationships, the resonance is quite simply lacking.

In this case it is best not to force things, and just move on to another tree, perhaps following an inner impulse, and find yourself welcomed by a different deva. If the maternal fir for example hasn't anything to give you, see how you get on with the cheerful ash... If all the trees are silent, though, you should move on and find a different forest.

Go further, deeper into nature, where a connection can arise with less interference. This going more deeply into nature will also have the effect of calming your spirit, so that it is easier for you and the tree to resonate together.

Do not try to force anything. Trying to force a tree in to communication by threatening it with fire, a saw or an axe is doomed to fail from the start. People really tried that. They got an answer actually, in the form of strange and very unpleasant, altogether physical resonances, which in some cases lasted for life or simply a branch on their noggin! Therefore, be loving in relating to your environment, to trees in this case.

How you shout into the woods likewise it will shout back to you![12]

---

[12] German proverb equalling 'What goes around, comes around.'

Portraits of different trees

What kind of tree is your World Tree? Fir, birch, oak or ash? Any of these can be regarded as the World Tree. For the Siberians the birch, combined with the fly agaric mushroom, is a possible stairway to the heavens.[13] For the Buddhists the Bodhi tree, under which the Buddha achieved enlightenment, is particularly worthy of reverence. Some Neo-Druids revere the oak above all. The toxic yew on the other hand is evergreen and bears red fruits in winter and a yellow fleece in spring, matching the description of the World Tree by the ancient Druids and the early Greeks.

Likewise, there is no 'good' or 'bad' kind of tree. Every species of tree has certain individual, as well as common features, which it shares within its family. The evergreen conifers for example have a warming tendency in winter.

In Germanic culture, the first human being emerged from the trunk of an ash tree, and Wuotan too hurt and offered himself, suffering in his unknowing pain, as a sacrifice on the branches of the World Ash until his power failed him and he had to let go, fell to the ground and in his new awakened form as Odin recovered wisdom, dignity and true legitimation to rule his kingdom.

As always in life's winding path expect the unexpected: if a yew turns out to give you advice on your love life, or a maple teaches you lessons in sweet temper, you should take it in your stride. More important than the expectations generated by book-knowledge is your personal attraction to and resonance with a particular tree. Perhaps a side of this tree that no book in the world has ever described before will be revealed to you alone.

To start with, following is a preliminary list of common mostly European trees along with their presumed properties. Of course, the location has its own influence, as have the whole circumstances of your dialogue.

---

[13] If you are not a Siberian shaman, you'd better steer clear of the fly agaric!

Alder

Alnus spp.

Kennings

Green alder: wren; Bran the Blessed; Embla (Germanic culture)
Brittle alder; bleeding tree; Morrigan or raven goddess;
Dana for the Celts; protection of warriors; shieldwood;
protection of the heart; guardian of the milk[14]

My own experience

The green, the brittle, the red and the black alder are all very different. The brittle alder does not like at all to be climbed upon. Its branches break easily into sharp spiky points like spearheads. It often occupies inhospitable locations with its roots deep in the boggy water.

Its energies are closely associated with storms and Samhain, the festival of the dead. Not surprisingly, it has a standing reputation as a witches tree.

The green alder, on the other hand, radiates a fresh serenity and lightness of spirit. It is comparatively small and can also be very warmhearted to children.

Note

Today children's furniture is often made from red alder wood, which does not seem to do the children any harm. On the contrary, it is a warm wood with a reddish colour, conveying a sense of security. Leaf tea made from the brittle alder is one of the countless remedies used for weaning.

---

[14] Milk churns were often made of alder wood, as it doesn't rot even when wet.

Alder buckthorn, glossy buckthorn, powder tree
Frangula alnus

Kennings
'Drop it!'; friendly to thrushes, particularly the fieldfare

My own experience
The glossy buckthorn, generally a bush or small tree with a number of stems, is in the truest sense of the word a person of coarse humour. Please forgive this uncomplicated vulgarity, but that's just the way it is, with the 'shitberry tree'. It helps excrete constipated stresses or inner demons that you have swallowed down, by an explosive process of voiding. Spiritually it can help you to purify your inner space and prepare yourself for a profound process of opening. For example, to get rid of an addiction or mania. If you want to rid yourself of something indigestible once and for all, simply try sitting under a powder tree.

Fieldfares are fond of the berries of the alder buckthorn, and they are also redoubted dive bombers: attackers by land and by air, they swarm at intruders and spatter them with precisely targeted deliveries of droppings before taking to flight. This of course is quite in keeping with the nature of the powder tree and its fierce reputation as "Killer of demons, witchcraft and poisons".

Notes
The stored bark is a drastic laxative as well. Its low-salt charcoal is good for making gunpowder. Both give rise to dramatic processes of evacuation.

A word of warning: the anthraquinone compounds of the powder tree that are active in the human gut can be quite toxic. The ingestion of the wrong kind of bark, bark that has not been stored or indeed of the leaves and the berries can lead to violent and potentially dangerous diarrhoea and vomiting. Do not experiment yourself with ingesting any part! The spiritual aspect is more than enough.

Apple
Malus spp.

Kennings
Auld Goggy's tree; health; healing; esoteric insight; rebirth

My own experience
The apple tree is a kindly loving teacher for children, a patient listener and keeper of secrets, as well as a guardian of youth under its mighty Lady Iduna and its good-natured guardian Auld Goggy. The latter flies on an owl and likes apple wine but doesn't approve the noise of tipsy gnomes. (Neither does his owl)

It's with us humans as with apples: Not the external appearance is what makes life's apple sweet but the ability to pass through the world with the lovingly astonished eyes of a child, without pride or prejudice. Only someone who bites through the carapace of the apple can perceive the sweetness of its interior. Only one who avoids being distracted by the sweetness gets to the core. Only when you look at the core very carefully do you realise the apple is a relative of the rose.

One who has understood this will always henceforth see the beauty of the rose in the apple and vice versa, as well as in many other plants. Are not human beings all different, and yet all brothers? That is one of the many teachings of the apple tree, the guardian of wisdom and of youth. It softens what has become hardened and gives plentiful wisdom to those who are familiar with the mystery of the pentagram. Plant an apple tree, and you will learn over the years to grow much after its kind. Three kernels contain the entire wisdom of the world.

Note
Yes indeed, 'Avalon' comes from the 'island of apples'. Not just for King Arthur, but for all older men as well (who may at times tend to look like grumpy apples) as well as women and children, fresh apples are highly recommended.

Ash
Fraxinus excelsior

Kennings
Yggdrasil; roofbeam of heaven; Ask; helper of horses;
equipment of warriors; glory of women; beauty competition;
spear wood; end of peace

My own experience
The ash is one of the most stimulating trees for the imagination and
immensely invigorating. It is the friend of all animals and craftsmen.
It uses its great intelligence in a very practical way.

For this reason, it can forgive an enormous amount, and can come to
feel at home in almost any new situation. Like a good craftsman, the
ash is practically impossible to kill. However often you cut it, it will
grow back again undaunted. Its motto is: 'Always straight on with
confidence!' Handles and shafts made from its wood feel pleasantly
cool in the hand, do not easily cause blisters, and though lightweight
are very durable. Even axes and wagon shafts were often made of ash
wood.

When its work is done, it likes to cool its feet respectively roots in water. Especially on a warm summer day, its leaves fluttering in the wind
dispense coolness and refreshment. If you need counsel to enable you
to overcome difficulties with enduring cheerfulness and trust, the ash
is the right tree to visit. If you suffer a minor injury at work, a com-
press of fresh ash leaves will be found helpful. Before picking the
leaves, as always, ask the tree's permission.

Note
According to ancient Germanic and Indian myths, man arose from the
ash. The tree as the analogue of the human being, the mythical World
Tree Yggdrasil of the Germanic peoples, is accordingly often seen as
an ash. Odin's spear Gungnir also had a shaft of ash wood.

<u>Aspen</u>, trembling or white poplar, quaking or golden aspen

Populus tremula

Kennings
Sharp wand; measuring stick of undertakers; exchange of friends; brother of birth; death; all things come to an end

My own experience
This is the tree of major leave-takings in life. Everything on earth is transient, and sooner or later it is time to take leave of something or someone. Sometimes death, a notice of termination or the loss of love takes away from us something to which we are so attached that it has become a part of us. The pain and the melancholy that follow from these voluntary or involuntary, anticipated or abrupt leave-takings, is just a consequence of our attachment to what has been lost.[15]

The trembling poplar can help us to detect this attachment before or after a loss in life and after an appropriate period of grieving let go of attachment and pain. Love and gratefulness remain...

As the beams of the sun dance on the waves, so the untroubled poplar, starting in May, lets all its attachments fly away into the sunlight in a cloud of dense fluffy seeds. Like sparkling rays of sunlight on the waves, its leaves flutter in the wind and encourage us to trust that at the end of our trials fulfilment is waiting.
This awareness gives a sense of deep peace in the here and now. It helps us to overcome an inner standstill and continue growing.

Note
As with other species of trees, there are several different subtypes of poplars, which in their resonating energies each differ a bit from another and communicative behaviour, but all still feel like poplars.

---

[15] Never cease to love: it is not the love but the attachment that causes pain. Love without attachment does not cause pain but admittedly is difficult to attain.

Bamboo

Bambusa spp.

Kennings
Swaying in the wind; equanimity; tallest of grasses

My own experience
There are more than a thousand different species of bamboo. All of them actually are grasses. Like reeds they grow unbelievably fast, and sway lithesome in the wind. They are hollow and very lightweight, but all the same practically impossible to break. If a gust of wind tears at them, they let it go by without much resistance, or else if necessary, bend down flexibly. As soon as the wind has gone by, they elegantly return to their original upright position. Good-natured as an old master, the bamboo observes the trials and tribulations of its environment. It never lets itself be stirred out of its inner calm. If you want to know what it feels like to stand up to powerful tempests without resistance by just letting them go by, then I recommend you resort to the cheerful serenity of a bamboo grove. The magic within it is often so powerful that even the inexperienced can sense a deep peace.

Even if the wind of life presses you down for long periods and persistently to the ground, you don't need to break. Gain inner freedom and nurture your stable elasticity with endurance, for example through LuJong, Tai Chi or Yoga. As soon as the opportunity offers, you will straighten up again of your own accord.[16] Attentive observation of the bamboo can teach you a lot about flexibility of form and the right kind of breathing during your exercises. Bamboo likes human beings, and generously gives them its wood for many purposes: as a building material, fibre, foodstuff and even for fuel.

Note:
Many species of bamboo even yield a bamboo leaf tea which has a very relaxing effect.

---

[16] If the pressure is unbearable, talk to the holly.
And then again sometimes it's better to strike the flag or make a stand at the right moment.

Beech, common, copper, European beech
Fagus sylvatica

Kennings
Tree of the twilight; letter staves; erudition; guardian of the sacred halls of Herne/Cernunnos; patient learning; academics' tree

My own experience
An ancient beech is a 'climax tree',[17] at the height of the wood's power. It is a primeval tree from before the Ice Age, which is reconquering its space at a measured pace. In its nature it is related to the nut tree, the chestnut and also the willow. It has a definite predilection for jays and squirrels.

It optimises its growth in youth, putting out a quickly growing, hanging whip shoot in spring, which only becomes upright in the course of the year. Therefore, it is a bit like an academic or scholar who during his youth studies patiently with bent back, without getting any profit from it, and only at a later age then becomes erect to his full height.[18] It is hardly surprising either that even in age the tree is well able to make use of the available resources, particularly light and water, in the best possible way.

Like a typical academic, the tree only becomes fruitful at a late stage. It then bears, especially in hot years, two little triangular nuts in each four-cornered seed head of the beechnut. The inner part of the beechnut is edible and, when eaten in moderation, as with practically all nuts, nurtures and fosters intelligence and the nerves.

The power of the beech can help us to find order and clarity in the hectic cacophony of everyday. It helps us with nowadays hysteric information overkill on the one, and with corporate thraldoms monotony on the other hand, enabling us to deliberately recognise what is beneficial in a given environment and use it for our own purposes of growth.

---

[17] Tree as part of the fully-grown, ancient hall of the wood.

[18] Do not forgo this second phase in your academic growth!

Benjamin fig, pencil-pusher's tree
Ficus benjamini

Kennings
In foreign surroundings

My own experience
This slightly toxic tree is normally found from Asia to northern Australia where it grows up to ten metres tall. It emanates sympathy for all office slaves who would rather be elsewhere, where they could grow bigger and more beautiful, rather than in the prison of their office, where they are kept small as a result of artificial boundaries.

It can teach us how to flourish in modest form, sustainably and persistently, in a prison of relative comfort, or else to grow to our true size independently, apart from the 'treadmill', in the free environment.

A word of warning – in freedom you need to face up to different challenges than in the office. Forming a realistic estimate of these is a matter for every individual. Whether as a potted plant in the office, where other people are responsible for your wellbeing, or as a mighty tree thrown on your own resources. It's a serious decision.[19]

Note
This has nothing to do with teamwork or the spirit of going it alone, but rather with the attitude to being dictated to from outside as against being responsible for yourself as a subordinate, independent but freely self-defined human being. Even an employee can feel him*her*it*whatever self to be a free person and behave accordingly.

---

[19] At least that's what my office rubber tree said. - I meticulously pondered hardships and benefits for a long time and never ever since regretted the decision to become self-reliant!

Birch, silver birch, warty birch, white birch
Betula pendula

Kennings
Dark grey skin; child of light; purity; tree of virgins; innocence; apprentice; student; shamans world tree; kidney tree; pioneer tree; feet in the water; sap stimulus; golden hair

My own experience
She stands fully relaxed with her beautiful white trunk and waves her leaves cheerfully in the wind like hair. Birches can teach us a lot about beauty. Though her trunk is smooth and white as innocence in youth, when birches get older, it becomes barky and almost black. But in the topmost branches, her face, she will always have the white gleam of a wonderfully beautiful, now fully mature beloved-one. It helps seekers for meaning and Druids at the start of their journey. When she is in her gorgeous golden autumnal dress, the highborn queen of the north reveals her beauty.

If you have quite practical questions about relationships or career, when you are just completely stuck, it will answer you in a 'tree-like' manner, and sometimes very directly. This can be painful at times, like the well-meant blow with a birch rod which 'awakens' the slumbering virgin. If you haven't ever talked to a tree before, the birch is a very good place to start. It relaxes, cheers, and with its innocence frequently puts people, even the most grumpy or solemn seekers, into a light and cheerful mood.

Note:
Many East European shamans hold so much trust in the birch that they even use it as the World Tree in their visionary voyages, climbing physically on it to travel the higher or lower spheres of existence. A cup of birch leaf tea, made from the young green leaves, is very healthy, relaxing and gets the juices flowing again. But don't pick the leaves without asking for permission, or the tree will be annoyed.

Blackthorn, sloe
Prunus spinosa

Kennings
Rose-Red; strongest of all red colours; sex appeal; hunger of love; beguilement; searching clouds; in duality with whitethorn; punk; Do it your own way; not letting oneself be kept in leading strings

My own experience
The blackthorn is a really strong rod for repelling evil spirits. It stands for proud independence and the ability to defend oneself. 'Stand your ground' pretty much sums it up. As a result, as any self-reliant being it has a powerful erotic appeal.[20] As it has mastered this level as well, it is the guardian of great mysteries. Its deva is a major teacher of supersensuous matters, in particular the ability to adumbrate past and future incarnations and accept them.

It is a wise teacher for mystical seekers and Druids, especially women. Be warned though: the kiss of mystical knowledge can easily burn your tongue forever. This is not a tree for the stupid.

Only after the first frost can its berries be eaten. Otherwise they are too young, as some people are, and still too bitter. Like some seekers on their first steps they are really full of bitterness before maturing to inner peace.

On our path through life we can't have only beautiful experiences. But viewed aright, the variety of our experience enables us to mature in love and understanding. The consciousness that even negative experiences can bring us closer to our final goal makes up one part of the blackthorn's wisdom. And what is our final goal? Not death, for sure. Go and ask a blackthorn. However, be advised: the answer could change you for ever if you can bear it.

---

[20] Like most plant beings, the spirit of the blackthorn knows no distinction between the sexes. It can appear in whichever sex it pleases.

Bodhi tree, pipal tree, sacred fig
Ficus religiosa

Kennings
Buddha's tree; tree of awakening[21]

My own experience
The nothingness of our vain attachments can be grasped particularly convincingly under this tree. There aren't any pockets in a shroud! In the same way old age, and finally death, takes from us our power, rank, standing, and even our physical body and present state of consciousness. The only thing that survives is the soul, along with the awareness and merit it has acquired through consciousness and the body.

Anyone who sits under a Bodhi tree, in full consciousness of the nothingness of apparent being, can really, in a few moments of rapture, have the same experience as the Buddha, the Awakened One, who sees through the illusion of temptations, and who became conscious of the one final reality of the omnipresence of the One in all being and all beings.

Notes
A word of warning: when you become aware of the nothingness of worldly, samsara-driven values, the effect may last for some time. Moving as a successful (and I mean this) awakened one, in a world populated by people who are imprisoned by temptations, then calls for an unbelievable amount of empathy. Otherwise it's just been a trip that you needn't have bothered with.

Offshoots of the first and second generation of the tree under which the Buddha achieved enlightenment are living today, one known by the name of 'Sri Mahabodhi' in Sri Lanka, and the other at the original place in India.

---

[21] In Sanskrit 'Bodhi' means awakening.

Box, boxwood, common boxtree
Buxus sempervirens

Kennings
Guardian of eternal rest; repose; security; constancy
separation and borders, especially between the living and the dead;
in China, 'long life'.

My own experience
A wonderful hedge tree for inner retreat, not just in monastery gardens. The box separates different things from one another. Its motto is: 'I keep only the most important. The rest I let go.' *Büchse* in German and box both come from the Latin Buxus. It has different effects depending on the location (for example in a herb garden, park or cemetery), and on the form in which it is cut. It patiently permits itself to be shaped into practically any form you like. It is adaptable and yet hard, and its hard wood is very suitable for turning.
It is very effective in getting rid of inner tensions and burdens from the past. Box helps us through the spleen, not just in matters to do with digestion, but also helping us in a spiritual sense to separate what is useful from what cannot be used. It is slightly toxic and helps as a stomach remedy and medicine for malaria. By supporting the processes of excretion, it also helps us to free ourselves from unpleasant recollections. In case of confusion, loss of orientation or nervousness caused by excessive stimuli, it helps you to separate the essential from the inessential.

Notes
I strongly advise you against the use and ingestion of the box, not just for legal reasons but because with this tree it can, in the most literal sense, end up in your pants. With the help of a box tree (if you just come in contact with a sufficiently big specimen), the excretion of emotional stresses or addictions may occur on a thoroughly physical level. Be careful when you are meditating. It attracts ants and flies in spring.

Cedar
Cedrus spp

Kennings
Survival; living in dignity despite the most difficult circumstances

My own experience
There are many different species of cedar. They are all extremely strong, and essentially related. Like a good queen, the cedar is aware of the cares of human beings living in its vicinity.

Even when faced with barbaric deeds, caused by obstinate idiocy that cries to heaven,[22] the tree offers all who come to it a constant refuge of serene peace and a space of repose in the arms of a loving queen. Compulsive complaining, self-righteousness and quarrelsomeness will be replaced by a fitting modesty, inner composure and the deep certainty of inner peace in the presence of true royalty.

He who has ears to hear, let him hear. He who has eyes to see, let him see. All those who have lost the thread of life, whether it has slipped or been torn out of their hands, can pick it up again through the power of the cedar. This inner focusing and recollection of the essential aspects of life makes the cedar an untiring messenger of love and peace among all beings.

Note
Many cedars live today in exile, scattered among parks and gardens around the world, where they can unfold their loving influence. A clever and loving being will always find a peaceful way of protecting itself from the consequences of other persons' ignorance, even if it means going forth into alien territory.

---

[22] Namely the ignorance which denies that all souls are always inseparably linked and part of the One. This makes all existing beings, whatever their form, nation, religion or race, brothers and sisters, whether they are conscious of it or not.

Cherry, bird cherry, sweet cherry
Prunus avium

Kennings
Freya's tree; sexuality

My own experience
Since time immemorial the cherry tree stands for joy in life, seduction and temptation, pleasure and courtly love. With its white flowers and very frivolous fruit, which it gives away freely, it is a patient teacher in matters having to do with sexuality, love issues and lovesickness. Right from the joyful innocent blossom to the pleasurably swelling cherry and the warm loving wood, the cherry consists of pure living virile energy.

Pregnant women and those who want to become pregnant can turn to the cherry for its blessing. It always acts in ways full of hope, delighting in life and in love. Like this it helps you to enjoy love pleasurably and free of guilt, without falling into the traps love may entail.

Should a love affair happen to go wrong, the cherry is a loyal friend who will listen with empathy and will then help you to find a love that does not entail suffering. As a man, you should adopt a gallant and polite approach to the cherry.

Even if you are a fundamentally unromantic and not-a-bit gallant nerd, you can still talk to the cherry tree as well. Grumpy or frigid people really should spend some time under the cherry tree. People who are too ill-natured to 'eat cherries with them', means who are unable to love, should be avoided, because love is not a crime. On the contrary: the perverse thing is to be a hypocritic lustpooper.

Note:
In Japan the cherry blossom festival is a time for enjoying life in the bosom of your whole family.

Chestnut, horse-chestnut
Aesculus hippocastanum

Kennings
Bread of horses; enemy of flies; concord; convivial gathering relaxation

My own experience
The horse-chestnut tree, an 'immigrant' of the distant past from the Balkan peninsula, is the classic tree for beer gardens. In keeping with the original quality of its homeland, it is a cheerful, self-confident, friendly rascal with a big golden heart for children, and a merry, nonchalant toper who enjoys beer and a hearty meal.

It is conscious of its own strength. Just its presence repels ill thoughts and flies, as well as petty killjoys and naggers. It shows how you can go through life in a relaxed way, with joy in friendship and concord. It liberates your thoughts from smothering anxiety about others and from obstinate incorrigibility.

It is notably friendly to children, as shown in old children's games like conkers or crafting little men and animals from horse-chestnuts.

Note
Both how to hold a pint, and enjoyment in moderation, can well be learned in the shade of the horse-chestnut's feathery leaves. It will repay senseless swilling with a well-earned hangover.

Quite in keeping with the tree's character, incidentally, ingredients are obtained from the horse-chestnut that are a remedy for boils and haemorrhoids.

Common hornbeam, European hornbeam, white beech
Carpinus betulus

Kennings
Niggardly; schoolmasterly; crooked growth; haggard
recalcitrant; restricting

My own experience
If a common hornbeam is allowed to be what it actually is, standing freely, perhaps groomed lovingly as the one depicted, it is an altogether charming personality. A healthy, unbent hornbeam may help people who have been repeatedly broken or forced to bend, and who therefore insist on their boundaries, to find the right measure of distance. On the other way around, it can help to see something good in or at least understand niggardly fellow human beings.

But if every new shoot has been bent and broken, in former times hornbeams would grow into a hornbeam grove or even hedge, an extremely impenetrable thicket which would keep out wild animals and undesirable persons, or at times even entire armies. Hard, crooked, unruly, pernickety like a desiccated governess, career hyena or some miserly teachers, it is then recalcitrant and distancing at the same time.[23] As for such bent or maimed hornbeams: I give them a very wide berth.

Note
To me personally, the common hornbeam is telling very little. With miserly hornbeam-like persons, decency will get you frustrated at best, as they only accept the rules, they go on making themselves. Best avoid them. If there is no other way, the best thing to fight them is with fire, be resolute and with real full force and resistance will soon be at an end.

---

[23] This applies analogously to the male equivalent, to misers, skinflints and curmudgeons.

Common walnut, Persian/English or Circassian walnut
Juglans regia

Kennings
hidden wisdom; the stone; quick apprehension; matured by life; shade in the heat; inviting resting place to doze; food for the brain; generous host; the colour brown; blackened wood; expeller of worms from the gut

My own experience
The walnut is the wise and generous host among trees, richly dispensing its many different kinds of gifts. The nutshells and leaves can be used as a dye for the hair or skin, or to tan leather.

Its nuts when enjoyed in moderation, are a 'food of the gods', for they support the growth of wisdom.[24] The walnut fosters strength of will and helps to make well-considered decisions. Under its protection, those who listen with an open heart find their mood stabilised.

Selfish pests, flies, nagging thoughts, grumblers and rash decisions find it difficult to coexist with the walnut though. Therefore, it is highly suitable for banning all the above even if it may be a painful experience for the ego. At the same time, it is a very understanding tree.

If you are prepared to do something for yourself, you will receive help. 'Stop railing and lift up your voice in the song for which it is intended.' For all who are willing to help themselves, the nut tree is a powerful opener of doors and bringer to pass of wishes, both in this world and in others.

Notes
The idea that there is a risk of dying if you fall asleep under a nut tree (provided there is no question of suicide attempts) is bogus.

---

[24] If you happen to be allergic to nuts please do not eat nuts.

Cypress, Sequoia, Redwood, Thuja, tree of life
Cupressaceae, Thuja spp. (see notes below)

Kennings
Tree of life. Thuja; conqueror of grief. Sequoia: risen from the ashes. Cypress: warmth after terror

My own experience
Although different species they are very similar in their way of helping to cope with death, misfortune and the end of things. They grant warmth in times of grief, creating calm in stillness and inner retreat. Restore calmness and balance to those who have lost everything. 'Life goes on. Leave death behind you and rejoice in life. Return from mourning to resume living.

Below the old crust of everyday, a new life is already waiting for you.' In this way the trees of life kindle trust, confidence and hope. 'Climb the steps of life, one by one, trusting in providence.' Just like the branches, extending one above the other right to the crown, even if certain beloved branches fall away.

The sequoias cones actually need fire, which destroys all the rest of the wood, in order to open. But then the seeds germinate quicker than all others. In times of great mourning they are ready to start sooner than other plants.

The cypress is the great dispenser of light, one that in its natural surroundings can also emanate the greatest warmth, when you have had a shock or suffered grief such that the blood feels almost frozen in your veins. Immediately following the loss, you would do well to get help from the trees of life. – Keep your chin up, life goes on!

Note
Cypresses, trees of life, sequoias and redwoods are very different species, but do all belong to the thuja family. In their nature and effects, they are all very similar.

Elder, Elderberry
Sambucus nigra

Kennings
Blushing with shame or rage; reddening of the face
glowing with anger; end and conclusion; the Norns
female trinity; the queen; Mother Hulda

My own experience
Mother Hulda appears in the elder in black (S. nigra), white (S. nigra var. albitida) and red (S. racemosa), like the three Marys trinity.

This can be a place where you meet gnomes, kobolds and other earth spirits. As a wishing tree, it frequently features as the mediator of wishes and requests. Mother Elder enchants and draws dark chthonic[25] forces to herself. She helps dark elements of the soul, like anger and such, find their way home, to Hel, that is to say.
But one who genuinely loves the tree will be loved and protected by the tree in turn. It may be very generous and healing to honest and well-behaved children in need. The elder values honesty, industry, uprightness and hard work.[26]

When it is treated with disrespect, Mother Hulda or Hel will come back at you with a vengeance. Elders like growing along sunny houses and stable walls and protect the inhabitants from all kinds of dark misfortune. To injure or even fell an elder brings really bad luck.

Note
Don't tie ribbons or wish lists too tightly, to avoid injuring the bark when the branch grows. Only properly cooked berries and flowers of the black elder are edible. But don't pick too many, because the elder needs the berries to attract birds, who pick off parasites. Elder tea can be a helpful remedy for sweating off cold infections.

---

[25] Dark, cold, earthy or subterranean powers. At times they may be helpful, wise, lovable and friendly, but most of them are, in all their very different ways, unfathomably deep, dark and chilling.
[26] Exactly as in the fairitale of mother Hulda: Do your duties with diligence and you become lucky.

Elm
Ulmus spp.

Kennings
Earth; Embla; cycle of growth; in its cold home; shroud of the lifeless; descendants of the seed; death and new beginnings

My own experience
The elm is a deep-rooted tree, and in fact often likes having its roots in water. According to Norse mythology, the first human woman emerged from the trunk of an elm. When confronted with apparently irresoluble problems, the elm helps us to get a clear view and resolve even really gordic situations. 'At the end of every night, morning follows, and every rain comes to an end.' When our inevitable end approaches, the elm reminds us that death, despair and defeat are often followed by a purified new beginning, free of all our ballast. In this way it allows us to transform the negative into the positive. Its deva is closely linked with the role of the strong, feminine and altogether sexual woman. An elm I know was profuse in its complaint about women losing their role as 'one of two sustaining pillars' of our society. They are 'not being initiated, but beguiled, defeminized, betrayed and exploited by the machine.' Which was evidently very painful to this Amsterdam's elm.[27] If you have problems in living out your feminine side harmoniously, with strength and devotion, ask the elm for counsel. That applies to emotionally emasculated men as well, by the way!!

Note
Its wood can be worked very easily and yet is sufficiently hard for carpenters and wood turners. A decoction of the leaves, moreover, is a helpful remedy for skin problems. The elm is threatened as a result of Dutch elm disease. Hope is offered by a resistant variety, 'U. hollandica' – likewise from Holland, a country where women are said to be strong and feminine at the same time.

---

[27] I abhor any macho posturing. Alas the elm just was extremely definite and to the point in what it had to say. What did it mean, by 'the machine'? Perhaps the metrosexual androgynisation of women during the misandric, but soon-ending Kali Yuga with its hatred of love and life itself.

Eucalyptus
Eucalyptus spp.

Kennings
Clarity; free breathing;[28] healing coolness; decongestant purification of skin and lungs; conqueror of fire

My own experience
Especially for cholerics among us, or those who are consumed by an inner fire of negative thoughts, I can warmly recommend spending time under an eucalyptus tree. Without any loss of its own power, it pleasantly cools the spirits and dispenses a redeeming inner serenity. If rage or hatred is making it impossible for you to think clearly, the eucalyptus can restore to you the coolness and clarity you need.

But a word of warning: don't abuse this clarity for the planning of evil deeds or homespun 'psychoanalysis',[29] either on yourself or on others, ere you will have to reckon with the gravest consequences. This is because the eucalyptus does not like absence of emotion, like the aquamarine or sapphire, it stands for crystal clear, cool clarity, but always with empathy.

Note
The trunk and the form of the leaves change from the young sapling to the mature tree. Young shoots close to the ground have a quadrilateral cross section and fleshy opposed leaves surrounding the stem. The older tree has a round trunk, and lance-shaped alternating leaves.

The eucalyptus itself is vulnerable to frost, but extremely resistant to fire: the trunk and the branches, with their etheric oils, are highly inflammable and will burn with a bright flame. Below ground, however, it has special roots which will start growing again at lightning speed after a forest fire. Its seed pods even need the heat of a fire in order to open.

---

[28] Particularly in connection with asthma, colds and hay fever.
[29] Trees contempt pseudoscientific jumbo-mumbo and psychotropic drugs.

Fig, common fig
Ficus carica

Kennings
Tree of Dionysus/Bacchus; tree of lovers; tree of the satyrs
bread of the poor

My own experience
Dionysus, also known as Philosykos (fig-lover) and Meilichios, brought humanity knowledge about the fig tree and the sexual organs. In former times, his gift made it possible for entire peoples in the Mediterranean region to survive the winter on dried figs.

Consequently, the fruitful fig tree, with its complicated mode of propagation, is regarded as a symbol of the acceptance of the blessings of faith in harmony with knowledge. It is the combination of ecstasy and logic: the fig can encourage us affirming life and love. Through the bodily relaxation and regulation of the lower two chakras, it's enabling us to accept sexuality gratefully as a gift, in which we rejoice and which we should cultivate, while at the same time we thankfully harvest its fruits.

On the other hand, it opens up to us ever-new and perpetually valid life-affirming paths, whereby we cheerfully cleanse ourselves of ideo-logical ballast as self-determining beings. It is the tree of true men and women. The 'fig sign' since ages is regarded as a clear indication of self-determined warding off of evil.

Eating figs gives both men and women a better relationship with their own sexuality. Especially when dried figs are soaked in water overnight, the thousands of small seeds also clean out the gut and strengthen the digestion.

Note
There is also decaffeinated fig coffee, which restores harmony in the stomach and let you get down.

Fir, silver fir
Abies alba

Kennings
Christmas tree
Aspect tree for Father Christmas, 'Oskar' or 'Father Frost'

My own experience
Like most European conifers, the silver fir is a very balsamic and comforting tree. Unlike the yew, it is nontoxic. Today it is favoured as a Christmas tree and generally associated with the Christmas season. This tree is very critical of civilisation and has serious problems with acid rain and other environmental toxins. It is often gnawed by wild animals and infested with fungi and bark beetles. Stress makes it age prematurely.

A healthy silver fir stands for the right point in life. Only when settling in the right place can it prosper and grow old. Then its roots often grow together in a brotherly way, and the tree becomes a constant refuge for denizens of the earth and root beings.
Its wisdom can be summed up as 'Plant no seeds in frozen soil'. Wisely choose the place you want to settle down, and which seeds you plant in a person's heart. In frozen or spoiled soil or hearts, even the best seeds will not prosper. The silver fir can show us the best way of dealing with carpers, biting criticism and an unhealthy environment: simply withdraw, avoid unhealthy places or people, for those who expose themselves for too long to a toxic environment are going to fall ill. This has nothing to do with misanthropy or running away from all your problems, it is just the logic avoidance of environments hostile to life.

Notes
The tree's resin is an effective remedy against colds, rheumatism and gum problems, and encouraging the perfusion of the blood. A pre-medieval formula for the healing of wounds is 'Liquid Gold', a mixture of equal parts of resin, honey and beeswax.

Ginkgo, maidenhair tree
Ginkgo biloba

Kennings
Grandfather-grandchild tree (Gōngsūnshù); temple tree
peaceful heart; gentleness of age; softness and gentleness
harmony

My own experience
The ginkgo is a living symbol of long life, endurance and adaptability
in general and of concord and peace in relations between man and
woman. Consequently, it is well suited to men and women who wish
for more balance in dealing with other people, and within their own
partnership.

It encourages your own thoughts and perceptions, fostering your own
attentiveness, the originator of your feelings, like a funnel in the form
of a ginkgo leaf, letting them eventually drop towards peace with
others. In this way it can help you retreat into your inner peace as well,
even at hectic times.

Note
It was only brought from Asia to Europe in 1730. Its seeds are
surrounded by a stinking husk, but they are nonetheless edible.
Pollination is carried out rather unique for a plant by mobile sperma-
tozoa. Goethe immediately was very fond of the ginkgo.

A ginkgo leaf extract that encourages the formation of acetylcholine is
an effective remedy against dementia. It contains many other ingredients beneficial to old age.

The temple tree in Hiroshima went up in flames following the American atomic bomb attack – and put out shoots again in the same year.

Grapevine
Vitis vinifera

Kennings
Bacchus; path of the voice; neck; strength of the back
greatest effort

My own experience
Wine is a gift to human beings from the childlike high-spirited god
Bacchus. Like a child, the vine needs the right kind of soil and the right
environment, with plenty of sun, in order to flourish in response to
loving cultivation.

One who knows the secret of its sweet berries holds the key to
unrestrained cheerfulness. But remember – *In vino veritas*, 'In wine
lies the truth'.

If you abuse it, you will learn that the serious-minded Saturn is also to
be found in wine – and see his rings circling before your giddy eyes!
Many a wise man has made himself an utter fool when drunk. In addition, many have become idiots through their jones to drink.

Addiction to drink, like any other addiction, is repulsive to the vine.
Knowing how to enjoy all things in moderation is what the vine is all
about.

Note
In his carefree childlike cheerfulness, and his inclination to sweets
and tiddly delights, Bacchus corresponds to some extent to the
Indian Ganesh.

Hazel
Corylus avellana

Kennings
Tree of grace; sweetest tree; nut of knowledge, master of a thousand thoughts and dreams, friend of children and songbirds; early childhood, magic and innocence of children; squirrels; hazel dormouse

My own experience
The hazel bush is a true friend of all children. It is a place where good fairies, gnomes and all kinds of helpful nature spirits are to be found. According to various ancient traditions, the hazel nut is the vessel of wisdom. The hazel nut helps children and adolescents in their sleep. Therefore, its shelter is also the ideal place to play or sleep for children of all ages. A hazel bush silences the thousand sorrows of everyday and replaces them with peaceful thoughts.

Under the hazel it is easy to get rid of nightmares. Which makes it especially suitable for children. Anyone who does not understand children should sit under a hazel shrub. The tree causes beaming child's eyes to open to the wonders, adventures and magic nature and a loving fantasy hold, even in adults.

What is more, you can make excellent bows and divining rods from the stem of the hazel. The leaves can be pressed, painted and so on. Ask the tree's permission first. It is an ideal tree for hanging wish ribbons or notes on. Likewise, ideal for fat balls, feeding stations or nesting boxes.

Note
Hazel leaf tea, together with enough time spent in nature and one or two hazel nuts per day, will be found beneficial for delicate children. Attention: Only provided no allergy is present and when taken in moderation, hazel nuts are good for child-development.

Hemlock
Tsuga spp.

Kennings
A mother's love; cuddling; warming; healing;
sinking into healing slumber

My own experience
Anyone who has nodded off peacefully under a hemlock tree knows what it feels like to be sheltered and secure. The tree gives tired people serenity, enabling them to switch off, let their gaze wander over the distance and feel they are protected. In my experience, this works best if you sit at the foot of a hemlock with your back to the trunk, and simply and deliberately relax.

Notwithstanding any interruptions, the hemlock surrounds you gently with its profound motherly peace. When you are very exhausted, you would do well to find a hemlock in the warm sunshine where you can sink into healing slumber. Unfortunately, freestanding hemlock trees are still quite rare in north-western Europe.

Note
The peace of the hemlock does not come from any narcotic effect, as with the willow, but rather from inner relaxation.

Its name comes from the fact that the rubbed needles of the western hemlock (T. heterophylla) have a similar smell to ground elder (Aegopodium podagraria), also known as goutweed. In assigning the name, the latter was then confused with the similar, deadly poisonous hemlock (Conium maculatum). The three plants otherwise have nothing to do with one another.

Hawthorn, whitethorn, quickthorn, thornapple, May-tree, whitethorn, hawberry
Crataegus monogyna

Kennings
Snow White; blushing virgin; terror; fearlessness; faces turning pale; friend of the blackbird

My own experience
The hawthorn is brave, inquisitive and joyful. 'Take heart and go forward courageously' is its motto. This Snow White can give young and old maidens the impulse they need to take heart and lay down their inhibitions, in a spirit of joyful love. Above all when sexual blockages are preventing human interaction. Openness is not a weakness, for despite being fittingly protected by its thorns, it is openness above all to which the hawthorn owes its inner and outer strength. With its glorious white flowers, it also stands for pardon, forgiveness and the cancellation of negativity. Honest love, not out of compulsion but from an open heart, without expectations or conditions, is an attribute of the strong. In this way the hawthorn can teach you not to let yourself be diverted from the path of all-embracing love and inner peace.

Hawthorn leaf tea frees you from inhuman pressure to achieve and strengthens the heart and love of oneself in young and old. For persons of mature age, it strengthens the heart, and often enough encourages a mild and gently matured love to blossom, making it possible for you to forgive yourself and others and so finally work your own redemption. A feelie or amulet made of hawthorn can help you in certain circumstances to get over traumas from early childhood, as well as mitigating the effects of extreme overactivity or underactivity.[30]

Note
To learn more, consider the fairy story of Snow White, as well as that of Snow White and Rose Red.

---

[30] You need to know about the nature of the hawthorn for this. Just draping a bit of wood round your neck is very unlikely to work.

Holly
Ilex aquifolium

Kennings
Tree of salvation; Winter King; rod of iron; the third of a wheel shaft; the third of a weapon; the pith of coal; endurance; taking things on oneself, acting deliberately without curtailing; Thor's appeaser; prickles only where necessary

My own experience
The holly is the residence of the Winter King, who generously distributes his gifts to the needy. As the 'tree of salvation', the holly tree is fully awake even in winter and is full of red berries. It's the ancients Christmas tree.

Even in unpropitious circumstances, it maintains a self-confident and trusting stance. Its wood can withstand an extreme frictive heat, as when used as the shaft of a wheel. In situations when there is no alternative, it bends in dignity under the cold load of winter but does not break. As soon as opportunity rises, it shakes off the snow straightening itself up to its former position.

Its leaves are equipped with prickles only up to one or two metres above ground level. In this way it protects itself against attacks from below. But higher up, where no attacks are threatening, it no longer wastes energy thinking about prickles.

If you are interested in learning an open attitude in relation to friends and enemies, while maintaining your own equilibrium the while, go and ask a holly. It will give you good advice against envious spirits and low persons and can tell you how to cultivate moderation in dealing with your friends. When the whole world seems gone cold and icy, even a little holly's sapling, knows how to stand by its ideals while at the same time remaining cheerful and balanced in oppressing circumstances, and rid itself of the oppression as soon as possible.

Holm oak, evergreen oak, holly oak
Quercus ilex

Kennings
Friend of boars; steadfastness

My own experience
The holm oaks I know are not given to big words. The tree embodies the Aristotelian ideal of upright self-sufficiency. In its essential nature, the holm oak can be placed somewhere between the holly and the oak. Therefore, the holm oak declines to shed its leaves in winter and has prickly leaves. For this reason, it is sometimes rather lonely, but does (in its grumpy way) welcome visitors.

When visited, it usually without words, passes on what it has to give: empowering sincerity, constancy, steadfastness and self-sufficient inner peace.

If you have a goal you believe in, the holm oak can help you with its unshakable strength to follow your path without laziness or distraction, trusting in future accomplishment, despite any familiar or new, almost insurmountable obstacles that you may encounter.

For one wise word of the holm oak states: 'When faced with the greatest difficulties do not despair but follow your path decidedly and securely.' In short, this tree helps those that help themselves.

Its near relative, the thick-skinned cork oak, is particularly resistant to fire. Holm oak and cork oak combine in themselves the defensive endurance of the holly and the resistance of all oaks, as well as the typical generosity to all who act with energy.

Notes
In Spain pigs are still fed in special holm oak groves today, known as *dehesas*. And on Corsica as well, domestic pigs that have gone back to the wilderness do very well under the many holm oaks. Freely given wood makes good wood for runes. When robbed from the tree, they turn against the evildoer or perpetrator.

Ivy, bindwood, lovestone
Hedera helix

Kennings
Field; greenest of all pastures; place for animals
satisfying the needs of many;[31] in competition with holly
clinging on; addiction; eternal life

My own experience
Not an easy tree to communicate with. Best try an ivy clinging to
a wall and not a tree being strangled, because the latter might be a
very unpleasant experience. Where a lot of ivy is growing, you can
prepare yourself to encounter the influence of Dionysus and Bacchus,
for the ivy has been associated with the gods of wine since time
immemorial. But the Muses, and their patron Apollo, may reveal
themselves to you through the ivy too. Like an over-solicitous mother,
or an addiction, which is but of limited use of the befallen tree but,
with its practically immortal clinging on, prevents it from being itself,
ivy climbs up its host.

At the same time, it is generous and offers good shelter and nourishment to many beings, from the bee to the thrush. If you listen carefully,
you will find in ivy a reflection of what hampers or holds you back, or
of your addiction, which probably is a flight from the real way of your
life. At the same time, you can learn from it a lot about loyalty and the
eternal life of the soul.
What a versatile, truly dignified tree, but only for those who know
how to go their way by themselves and without drugs. Be warned: all
others will just have drifting, clinging thoughts under its influence.

Note
Ivy is toxic. Taken in very small quantities, it relieves cramp and can
serve as an expectorant. Certain of its components may kill breast can-
cer but are allergens. So do not experiment yourself.

---

[31] Starlings, thrushes, robins and many other songbirds and insects.

Juniper, common juniper
Juniperus communis

Kennings
The beautiful warrior; Baldur's tree; peace in oneself
overcomer of discontent

My own experience
The juniper is an unerring and powerful champion of the bright cause.
Often it is a safe refuge for the souls of the dead, before they go on to
enter the Sea of Souls.

It is defensive, and even toxic, but it gives its gifts to those who take
the time to attend to it. It instantly drives away all kinds of demons,
delusions and bad moods. A few dark berries of the juniper banish
anger instantly. Equally effective is fumigation with a few needles.

If you listen carefully, the tree can teach you to find calm in the storm,
to go soul-searching and find peace in yourself.
It can help you to recover your own roots and as a result to anchor
yourself in a stable and balanced way. Here the juniper has a modest
mode of action, not using big words but conveying a sense of deep
inner peace.
Even those who are tired of life itself can recover with the help of the
juniper, for it teaches us to allow ourselves time and rest independently of outer circumstances.

Notes
Juniper berries soothe the skin, liver and wind, as well as all kinds of
anger. This is because anger is just a flatulence of the brain wanting to
get out. Whatever you do, only use the two-year, old blue berries, and
these in small quantities, otherwise they can be toxic. Gin is made
from juniper, but due to the high content of alcohol inefficient to calm
an upset mind. On the other side the berries are very good in sauer-
kraut to prevent flatulence.

Kaki, Japanese persimmon
Diospyrus kaki

Kennings
Superfluity in the desert; trust; taking time to mature; joy in life

My own experience
The kaki is an unbelievably cheerful tree! In China and Japan, it has been cultivated as a fruit tree for millennia. In Europe you'll only come across it in just a few botanical gardens. This jolly and deeply wise chap alone is a good reason for revisiting a botanical garden.

When young the fruits may be somewhat bitter, but when fully matured they are incredibly healthy, being a rich source of provitamin A for instance, and beneficial to the stomach if you have diarrhoea.

Through the tree or the fruit, you are empowered to really believe in miracles and unshakable joy in life. Its message in short is: 'While waiting, trust in yourself and then go on your way full of good cheer.'

In China it is called the 'Tree of the Four Virtues', because it is a long-living, pest-resistant, shade-giving nesting place for birds.

Notes
The kaki fruit is so charged with all kinds of vitamins and the energy of the mother tree that I recommend it despite the long transport route, as a way of keeping up your vitamins in winter.[32] It is said to have healing properties for stomach disorders, cough and prepared correctly curing some forms of headache, high blood pressure and fever.

---

[32] The environmental foorprint arguably as with all tropic fruit is really bad, but scurvy is not nice either. Ponder and decide wisely.

Kauri, New Zealand Kauri, Dammar
Agathis australis

Kennings
Tane Mahuta; do it your own way; stand up and be a man!

My own experience
The 'Lord of the Forest', Tane Mahuta, stands in New Zealand. It is the biggest of all kauris which, according to a Maori legend houses the consciousness of an exceptional dweller: the creator of our world. As a true New Zealander, this tree is a real warrior and a wise though good-humoured counsellor at once. In a creative way, this giant tree always looks for the most peaceful possible solution. But, when no other solution is to be found, it does not shun conflict either. The kauri values people who overcome obstacles and grow beyond themselves by persistence and thought. Its will to survive and wealth of ideas are without parallel. Not surprising endurance is the characteristic of the children of Tane Mahuta.

If you are looking for happiness, ask a kauri. Don't fret about the answer: the solution might involve several laborious steps. If one step seems to difficult, just ask, and the kauri can awaken the solution sleeping within you. The caring love that the kauri brings to us human beings is almost endless. It has an open ear for practically any problem and is a constant source of inspiration as well. But you will need to exercise patience, for the kauri thinks long and hard before coming up with a solution – which it always does. 'Let me think...' is one of its seeds of wisdom. Before it enters a state of deep thought, sometimes for days, before sending its inspiration.

Note
Caution: don't tread on the roots. They are just below the surface, and very sensitive. Communication can easily be carried on from some distance. In Europe you find it in the hothouses of botanical gardens.

Larch
Larix decidua

Kennings
Blessed white or wild Ladies; the wise virgins; gentleness
discarding of pain; letting go; dissolving hardness; trust
faith in God; gentlest of the conifers; midwives' tree

My own experience
The 'Blessed Ladies' have been known to often take up residence in a
larch. These are powerful, practically angelic beings offering care and
protection in all matters of concern to women. They can help you to
let go of your hardness, even when it is a response to the hardening of
others, and so restore failing courage and reenable the energy to live
your life.

The larch helps to accept without resignation the unavoidable and inevitable losses without quarrel or judgment. It helps in such a way
that you do not suffer any abiding damage yourself. It aids with the
heavy daily grind when it seems unbearable, making it possible for
farmers' wives, housewives or mountain women in particular to adapt
flexibly to their situation into old age, with gentleness and charm, and
to go their own way with self-respect in all weathers.

Even a cruel loss often means the gain of freedom. Seeing these
opportunities and accepting life in complete understanding is the
power of the larch. Nevertheless, when a situation is senseless, it
opens up new paths for you and gives you the strength to pursue them
in a well-considered way, and as gently as possible. Treading new
paths can call for a lot of courage, strength and hard work. Weigh the
alternatives well and decide in the spirit of gentleness with the larch's
help.

Note
The larch can cope with a broken crown better than other conifers,
because it adapts itself to every new situation. Therefore, it is the only
conifer to shed its needles in winter.

Laurel, bay tree, ornamental laurel
Laurus nobilis et al.

Kennings
Fame and glory; power and prestige; magnanimity; dignity

My own experience
As an expression of fame and glory, the laurel wreath has been legendary since the antique world of Greece. Perhaps people put it on the heads of victors just to prevent them suffering from dangerous megalomania. For when you come to understand the laurel, you get a sense of something almost impossible for humans: remaining magnanimous when in a position of power.

If you happen to be plagued with indecent impulses of whatever kind, go sit under a laurel, as it encourages clear and pure thoughts. It offers those who are receptive a certain protection against impurity in their thoughts and actions, especially when they come to power. Having power and dignity also means having many enemies, envious spirits and the burden of responsibility. This is just where the laurel comes in helpful, enabling you to maintain dignity in the light of your own power. At the same time, it gives you a certain inner and outer integrity, as well as the capacity to endure, and protection against vulnerability. As a result, it encourages self-confidence and the ability to see things through in magnanimous action.

A word of warning here: anyone who makes his own laurel hedge too high as a boundary, in the form of snobbery or through being stuck up, can find himself feeling lonely behind it. While one who rests on his laurels for too long and falls victim to the temptation of laziness will find them withering on his head.

Notes
The nymph Daphne fled from the attentions of the god Apollo by taking the form of a laurel. As a sign of his undying love of her, Apollo has worn the laurel wreath ever since. Ornamental laurel is not suitable for use as a seasoning, but its energies are similar.

Lemon
Citrus x limon

Kennings
A sour taste makes a merry mood; sourness contracts; refreshment

My own experience
The lemon, like all citrus fruits, induces a Mediterranean atmosphere just when you look at it. The original, unadulterated, cheerily refreshing mentality of the south is part of their nature, just like their aversion to cold.

All edible citrus fruits are cultivated forms, often farmed in modern slavery in massive monocultures. In a way the lemon makes me think of an immigrant worker from the south, who is trying to earn a living in a cold and alien clime, but still hopes to be able to return to his beloved homeland someday, although he goes on being oppressed.

Let's not forget to mention there are some very hard and thorny species of lemon, like the Korean lemon for instance.

Notes
Orange, clementine, mandarin, grapefruit, pomelo and how many more – they all result from breeding and crossing of the original Citrus. In their essential being they are quite individual but taken all in all very closely related to one another.

Lilac
Syringa spp.

Kennings
Friend of all butterflies;
peaceful, modest delight in life without frivolity;
arts; dance; music; the finer pleasures of life

My own experience
Where the gentle scent of the lilac is in the air, you can let your soul
hang loose in a cloud of butterflies.

The lilac most resembles a distinguished *grande dame*, of quality, style
and mature good-natured charm.

It blossoms unexpectedly in warm, but often barren locations, and
persistently attracts a colourful swarm of cheerful butterflies, as if
inviting them to a dance.

Lilac can teach you a lot about unobtrusive quiet influence from the
wings. For people who want to realise their goals with style and a
certain level of quality, the lilac is an ideal mentor.

This may but does not have to involve artistic activity.

Note
Lilac grows very well on all bare, sandy and stony surfaces, managing
to turn such areas into a scented shelter for butterflies in a short space
of time.

Some envious plonkers call it invasive... Every species once was
invasive! 'Do not try to push against the wheel of time.

'Ride it in grace while it swells and transform the given into the beautiful.'

Linden, lime, basswood
Tilia spp

Kennings
Nurture of a healer; clothing of a healer; herb tree
healing from inside; gentleness; coming to equilibrium
appeasement; peacefulness; relief of all evil; a judge's mild advisor
gentle forgiveness; love dancing; soothing; peace tree; inner peace;
love in the heart; soothing of heat

My own experience
Just the presence of a linden puts you in a mild and gentle mood,
having a soothing and cooling effect on inner tension and disharmony.
Forgiveness and inner peace lead to peace in the outer world.

The linden helps you not to pass judgment on yourself or others, but
to forgive wherever possible. 'Always heal, never injure' is one of the
linden's dicta. And following: 'Let things remain in peace as they are,'
'Let people be as good as they are' and 'Only help if you can do so without injury'. As the court linden in former times it even helped judges,
and today it still helps anyone to avoid passing unfair judgments on
themselves or on others, for it soothes and appeases those who give
way to anger and the desire for revenge.

As the dance linden it invites you to join in peaceful dancing, and
brings together people of all groups, ages and sexes in its circle.
Under the linden is the perfect place to practise dance, LuJong,
Tai Chi or yoga and find one's equilibrium. According to tradition, it
protects against lightning and demons. Therefore, on account of all
these good qualities it is often planted to celebrate the birth of a first
child.

Note
The 'robe of a healer' refers to linden blossom tea, which soothes
many ailments, as well as to linden bast, which can be woven into
fabric. Every part of the linden has its healing powers.

Maple
Acer spp.

Kennings

The craftsman's tree; master of forms and colours

My own experience
From the Japanese ornamental maple to the Canadian sugar maple, a maple tree, like a good craftsman, can feel at home in practically every situation. However often you prune it, it comes back again undaunted. The way things are, that's fine for the maple, it accepts whatever comes and makes the best of it. It even celebrates autumn in a merry colourful display of its leaves. Though not before it has let its winged seeds go out into the whole world.

With this mentality it helps to find satisfaction in craft activities and the seemingly dull duties of everyday life. It was always the classic wood for spindles and knife handles. Since time immemorial the maple has provided outstanding wood for working tools. It sits well and feels pleasantly cool in the hand.

But not only does it cool externally, it also alleviates the heat of internal conflicts. It can show you how you can have a look at an inner or outer conflict from an independent perspective not marred by negative emotions and in quite a new way, so that perhaps you may be able to make something out of it. It's not a prissy tree, but of a cheerful, honest to goodness and down to earth kind. Don't be surprised if it gives you its opinion without mincing its words – just like an honest and enlightened master craftsman playing with forms and colours.

Notes
Maple syrup is a wonderful sweetener when you have a cold. Unlike cane sugar or honey, its sweetness has a gentle aroma of vanilla.

Mistletoe
Viscaceae; Santhales; Loranthaceae; Verbascum ssp.

Kennings
Godly semen from above; youngest of all trees;
innocence; Baldur's trial; peace love and understanding

My own experience
You just have to kiss under a mistletoe sprig! – Then feel true love,
embrace life and do a whole lot more than just kiss, as the symbolism
of the white and sticky berries points clearly to the seed of the gods
fallen from heaven. It is the godly seed which fathers the child of light
in innocence anew every year. Men and women with deficient libido,
or having problems in connection with ejaculation, potency or fertil-
ity, are advised to turn to the innocent and cheerful wisdom of the
mistletoe.

The light god Baldur was shot with an arrow made of mistletoe by a
fiendish ruse of Loki. There are Druids who claim that Baldurs mother
Frigg forgave the innocent mistletoe for the death of her son. Through
forgiveness was the light god then reborn out of the deepest darkness
in the midst of winter, as a new area's child of light. These same
sources are familiar as well with the secret word of universal love,
which the mature Odin whispered in the ear of his beloved dead son
on his last voyage, like this making it possible for him to return again.
This is the master key for overcoming the coldness of the world. That
is where the main strength of the mistletoe lies. Smallest of all, youngest of all, mightiest of them all!

Notes
The slightly toxic mistletoe lives on other trees. There are several
species which only favour certain host trees and are very heavily
influenced by them.[33] In our parts there are the pine mistletoe, the
spruce mistletoe and the deciduous mistletoe of the genus Viscum.
The oak mistletoe even belongs to the Verbascum family.

---

[33] In Central America there is even a tiny mistletoe that grows on cacti.

Oak
Quercus robur

Kennings
Revered by craftsmen; work of the carpenter; highest of all shrubs
Zeus tree; Thors tree; power; endurance; gnarled strength
mastery; rest and peace; friend of the boar

My own experience
Oaks tend to be strong, fundamentally solid, knotty and heavy trees. Their thick, bitter bark is suitable for tanning. The same time the oak is a friend of pigs, jays and squirrels. Oaks are usually not very talkative, but they do tolerate the presence of visitors. You should try to speak to them when they are – or perhaps better, when 'he' is – in a particularly good mood, sometimes signalled by a rustling of the leaves.

Like an old druid or matured warrior, oaks love children, birds and little animals. To them thy generously gift their acorns.

The oak maintains its inner peace and strength by rarely interfering with the business of others. But they help people suffering from the effects of mental or physical violence.

Hurt people often develop a rough outside, a certain hardness and become grumpy. The oak helps us to understand that 'Under the effect of violence all that is hard, can only break' It teaches in what situations we need to be hard, enduring and bitter, and how much more satisfying it is to give away one's acorns whenever possible in a spirit of loving generosity. As a result of this mature wisdom, the oak is the patriarch of the trees in a position of achieved power. It has always been the tree of Thor, of Cernunnos and Zeus. It is the tree of the oracle of Dodona. However, it also teaches in a more or less serious way, through the acorns in particular, what consequences amorous escapades can have. – Even for ancient gods: 'Be careful who you give your acorns to.'

Olive tree

Olea europaea

Kennings

Friend of the peaceful; tree of peace; hope of peace; deep peace;
Sermon on the Mount; matrimonial bed of Odysseus; atonement;
wise repose

My own experience

In all cultures the evergreen olive tree is regarded as a symbol of
lasting peace. It stands for the realisation that all human beings are
children of a single father, even if they pursue different paths.

As in the case of the fig and the vine, cultivation of the olive is thought
to have been a gift of the gods, in this case Neptune and Athene.
Jesus Christ also preached peace and the one commandment to
humanity on the Mount of Olives, in an olive grove. The dove which
brought Noah an olive branch as a sign of peace is still the archetypal
symbol of peace between nations today.

Even Ulysses based his enduring will on the peace of this tree, for he
made his marriage bed directly out of a still rooted olive tree.
Like Wuotan/Grimnir, this gave him roots, strength and the inner
calm needed to finish his seemingly never-ending odyssey and truly
come home. Inner peace, and the understanding that peace is the
natural state of humanity, is something you can apprehend from the
olive tree. Each of its main branches, incidentally, can be assigned to
one of its main roots, for 'As above, so below; as within, so without.'
Peace and repose within ourselves is a condition of peace in outward
action, and vice versa. Only one who sows peace can reap it.
'Peace be with you.'

Notes

Symbol of the atonement between Neptune and Zeus.
Neptune/Noah(tun), Lord of the Tritons, values peace on earth higher
than the final victory over Zeus. Later curiously found as the gift of
Athene, daughter of Zeus, to the Athenians in competition with
Neptune for the position as patron of the city.

Pear
Pyrus spp.

Kennings
Girl tree

My own experience
The fruit of the pear has something watery, moist, bloated about it. The tree itself helps slightly distraught persons, or people who easily get weepy, to centre and stabilise themselves and gather strength from their own inner peace.

It helps weak little girls to grow into big strong girls who are not weepy but happy, big girls who, like the pears wood do not lose their countenance or form easily. Maybe that is why in early times the tree was not a particular favourite of the roman catholic clergy. Just sitting under a pear tree when it is in full blossom, on a sunny day in early summer, can give you deep peace in and from the depth of your being.

Note
Possibly the tree may be able to help people with dropsy and problems of the lymph system. Above all in the form of dried fruit or pear bread, in place of fat and sugar.

The pear was cultivated even before Celtic times all around Europe. Romans especially liked it for food and medicine. As certain men tend in old age to an 'apple form' (limp apart from the belly), so some women tend to a 'pear figure' (limp apart from the backside). Possibly having recourse to a pear tree may shed light on the situation, and get the juices flowing again.

Hildegard von Bingen was probably a stern visionary but not a happy girl, as she didn't have a good word to say about the pear. Maybe she should have given them a try…

Palm
Arecaceae, Palmae

Kennings
Daughter of the winds; dispenser of shade; refreshment of the eye; home in the desert

My own experience
There are many different kinds of palms. Not all of them bear dates or coconuts. But with their widely waving branches they all dispense shade in the blazing sun. In their original homeland they often indicate the presence of water: a place where people can meet up, rest, replenish their energy and relax.

To really experience what a palm feels like you had to go into the desert, where they offer refreshment to the eye after endless monotony. Even in our concrete urban deserts they do still offer an intimate space to relax in.

The tropic coconut palm has a quite similar yet fundamentally different resonance. They are born optimists and easy-takers, witty seafarers and pioneers – true Polynesian heroes!

I do not recommend meditating under a coconut palm bearing nuts though. Getting a whole coconut on the bonce may make see you the stars dancing before your eyes but is a painful and potentially fatal experience. 'No jokin man!'

Notes
In some countries, spitting date stones into the wind is regarded as disrespectful – both to the palm and to the wind.

Plane, maple-leaved plane or London plane
Platanus x acerifolia

Kennings
In rank and file; collective; strong through obedience;
a good salary and well-deserved retirement after duty

My own experience
The plane is extremely frost-resistant, and it is almost unaffected by exhaust fumes and compacted soil. This makes it an ideal tree for cities and boulevards. It was created in London in 1650, on the eve of the industrial revolution, by crossing an American and an oriental plane. Often confused with the craftsman's tree, maple, it is similar to the latter in nature. But by contrast with the maple, the main emphasis for the plane is on working in a controlled collective of many persons in industry, or in factories, the military, the police or big companies for example. It is quite astonishing how much smog, fine dust and toxic substances the plane can tolerate. All the planes I know personally moreover share a sympathy for technology, machines and industry, as well as a predilection for marching music. Quite a unique feature among trees!

Planes like standing in rank and file, on an avenue, where they can quickly pass on strength to workers just by touching them, enabling them to give diligent service, and helping pensioners to enjoy their well-deserved retirement. Their fruits are small cylindrical nuts which cling closely together in a collective cluster even after the leaves have fallen, forming balls which hang from the branches.

Note
The urban tree par excellence! Somebody once painted two hands on the trunk of a plane tree, at shoulder height, and wrote 'Human charging station' below it. If you are living in the city, the plane is an ideal tree for beginners. Don't expect any deep and meaningful dialogue, but you can look forward to being properly 'charged up'. Just putting your hands on the trunk is generally all it takes.

Plum, damson
Prunus domestica (spp.)

Kennings
Old prune; new youthfulness

My own experience
The plum of whatever variety from damson to greengage releases tensions and resultant illnesses of all kinds with its gentle cooling effect. In China it is, along with the bamboo and the pine, regarded as one of the 'three friends of winter'. Anyone who, either in the flower of youth or the maturity of age, suffers from excessive or deficient sexual activity can obtain wise counsel from the plum. If it is not a case of traumatisation, the plum tree can help you, especially in the blossoming and fruiting phase, to detect tensions in this area and resolve them.

The ancient Roman Marcus Valerius Martial poet wrote: "Take plums for the brittle burden of age, for they tend to release the tensed abdomen." Quite wise: fresh plums have a laxative effect. They can help when the lower abdomen has got itself in a tangle, as well as healing stomach disorders. Dry plums, so called prunes soaked in water have a gently laxative effect when you have been unwell, or when you have a sensitive stomach. Don't ingest plums (and this applies to all stone fruit) along with water, or it can give you the squitters. In view of its high borate content, moreover, the plum is thought to be effective against osteoporosis and senility. Plum puree can also raise the spirits, even without lengthy boiling. You must remove the stones first, as they contain prussic acid.

Notes
Probably one of the oldest cultivated plants in the world, known to the Mesopotamians more than 6000 years ago as the *armanu*, plums came into our culture by way of Armenia. The plum is said to have been systematically introduced by Charlemagne.

Slivovitz is a brandy largely consisting of plums and carries the energy of the fruit. - Enjoy in moderation!

Quince
Cydonia oblonga

Kennings
Gift for newlywed; Venus in possession; Iduna's secret
golden apples or yellow gold of the Hesperides

My own experience
Iduna's secret is the knowledge of eternal youth. This can only be achieved, and not consumed, through your own wisdom, even if one can write it down: beauty and youthful vitality are not so much dependent on the years and the wrinkles in the peel, as on the inner willingness to work on yourself into ripe old age, with diligence, love and devotion, and let the love so acquired appear outwardly so that it is visible to your next.[34] The quince teaches us the power of hard work and of love that is patient and sincere.

Notes
When asked by their children for advice, aged mothers have often tested potential sons or daughters in law by the following method, to judge the quality of their diligence and loving commitment:
Give a person quinces. If you get quince jam or jelly back from them, you can conclude that they value you, that they are hardworking, grateful and generous.

---

[34] To your next, the person nearest to you. Mostly you have to decide who is your next. This doesn't have to encompass the whole world and the entire burden of humanity.

Robinia, locust, black locust, false acacia
Robinia pseudoacacia

Kennings
Noble solitary warrior; a light in darkness; city tree; pioneer tree; wood of heroes and dwarves; upright oak of the Native Americans

My own experience
The robinia comes originally from northeast America, and still shows a strong connection with the Algonquin tribes who inhabited the region in former times. As the 'upright oak of the Native Americans', the robinia represents the ideal image of the noble solitary warrior, far away from his own homeland. Its tough wood used to be favoured for use in mines, as it sometimes shines in the dark and gives warning shortly before it is about to break with a loud cracking sound. This of course is very much to the taste of any dwarf, to whom it is known as 'hero wood'.

The robinia is not as grumpy as most oaks, but all its parts are poisonous. Definitely a pioneering tree, on account of its beautiful blossoms, it is often cultivated in parks. If you feel powerless and feeble in your environment, ask the robinia for advice. It can show you how to lead your life proudly, equably and without reproach in ethical or moral terms. The robinia is a C4-plant, independently capturing the nitrogen it needs from the air and at the same time fertilising the soil. The ideal tree for city Druids, then, living like the Native Americans in the midst of urban 'excessivilisation' and in alien surroundings, who want to lead successful and fulfilling lives without comprising their integrity.

Note
The robinia is an 'immigrant', and its presence has influenced our ecosystem. This is termed anthropogenous evolution. You can either try to stem against the wheel of time or, if you don't want to be crushed beneath it, surf on the wave. For further wisdom considering the big wheel of fortune and time listen closely to the 'Carmina Burana' by C. Orff.

Rose, wild rose, dog rose
Rosa spp.

Kennings
Sleeping Beauty; pain of love; sleep of thorns; the defending virgin protection against impetuous admirers

My own experience
One who understands the rose knows how to love! The rose helps lovers of both sides through times of romantic storms and troubles. Like roses, people too are on a path of development from the promising bud to the mature hip.

As Walter von der Vogelweide long ago observed, one mustn't break off a rose or touch it against its will, or it will wither. But before that the rose will prick the perpetrator so painfully that he will feel the searing hurting going deep to his marrow. When you talk to them nicely, however, they will continue blossoming for a long time. If you treat them well and give them your genuine love, they will produce even more beautiful flowers. If you have been scorned by a thorny rose, you should learn something from the experience and go on to the next one – for there are thousands of different roses. Some are just a bit vain, others full of thorns. Others flower beautifully for a long time. Others again blossom quite modestly, and just want to be discovered and loved, but then they may surprise you with a tenderness, which makes you forget all toil and weariness.

Nevertheless, take advice: there are some cruel roses that first entice you with brightly coloured blossoms and promises, only to later imprison you in a horrid tangle of thorny briars. The cultivation of love with all its thorns and flowers, raising it from the wild rose to the perfection of the cultivated specimen, is an art in which many have found fulfilment.

Note
The above applies not just to women, but to men as well.

Rosemary, anthos
Rosmarinus officinalis

Kennings
Rose of the sea; granter of milk; remembrance of veterans
gentle heartfelt warmth; warms the body to the bones;

My own experience
Admittedly it is usually a rather small tree, but what a healer it is!
Chewing a few of the needles cleanses the mouth. The scent relaxes
and conveys the sunny warmth of the south. It gets all your glands
gently producing again, even if they are blocked or hardened.
Any new mother can increase her milk flow significantly by chewing
a few single rosemary needles. Irritating nodes and obstructions of
the milk flow in the breasts can also often be resolved by chewing a
few single rosemary needles.[35]

With its stored solar energy, it wards off various illnesses and makes
it easier for you to digest fat. In combination with physical exercise, it
contributes to the rapid dissolution of accumulated fat and toxic
blockages in the body, so they can be sluiced out of the system.

It also helps us to dissolve and let go of spiritual hardening and
ancient dross through gentleness and warmth of the heart. It has the
most powerful effect in its natural southern habitat, where it can grow
to considerable size. Cruelty and coldness are the only things it
dislikes. Faced with these, it withdraws.

Notes
Sage, who has an inhibiting effect on the flow of the glands, is its
opposite and partner not only in the kitchen.

---

[35] Do not try any spice carelessly because if consumed excessive or too concentrated as an oil
it may have toxic effects, even faster for babies and unborn. Rosemary may lead to premature
birth. Avoid or use very moderate during breastfeeding and to be on the safe side avoid during
pregnancy, like most strong spices.

Rowan, mountain ash

Sorbus aucuparia

Kennings

Delight of the eye; joy and food of animals; friend of all songbirds; invoker of spirits

My own experience

Rowans are frequently found standing in hedges or at the edge of a wood. With their gleaming red berries, they are a delight for the eye and loved by many species of songbird.

Consumed in moderation, the berries help to purify the soul, spirit and body. If you eat too much or in greed, you will get a very solid stomach ache. 'Sometimes less is more'.

The rowan can pass on this insight into moderation, together with kindling an untrammelled joy in life from the heart of your being. It shows us how to live joyfully in the actual moment and spot, without worrying about supposed securities.

Perhaps this teaching has something to do with the birds, which like to cavort in the rowan tree cheerfully and without any cares. The rowan tree was used as an oracular tree in former times. Listen carefully to what it has to say – perhaps even a bird may have a message for you...

Note

In return, the birds distribute the seeds of the rowan at their favourite sitting places, in hedges and on the edge of woods. Just to observe the coming and going of the rowan's feathered friends in the tree can be quite fascinating.

Scots pine, Pine

Pinus sylvestris, ssp.

Kennings

Resin pine; torch tree; resinous tree

My own experience

There are more than one hundred and eleven pine species which vary widely depending on their growth, the species itself and the location. With pines, it is very much a matter of where and how they grow. A mountain pine in the vicinity of high mountains will call forth different thoughts from a tall pine in the wood. Nevertheless, they all share the fundamental character features of warm, balsamic femininity.

A pine does not shed its needles neither in biting frost nor in scorching heat. Pines are protective evergreen trees, which can teach you how to make the best of a situation even under the nastiest conditions.

It is a very caring and balsamic tree, with a lot of warmth, which it gives off in winter with perceptible effect on the surroundings, as well as in its resin. Because of the resin, pine wood takes fire easily and burns with a bright flame. With their warmth and their brightness, they can often shed light on your path.

Note

In keeping with their nature, pines help against cold attacks. Chewing the needles disinfects the mouth. When you have a cold, pine tip syrup is a useful remedy. The resin, with just a few exceptions, has a warming, brightening and beneficial effect in salves or in fumigation.

Just the scent of pine resin can help you to relax and replenish your energy. As its wood takes fire easily and has a pleasant scent when it burns, it was used in former times as pine kindling for illumination and for lighting fires.

Service tree, elf tree, chequer tree, Swiss pear, dysentery pear
Sorbus torminalis

Kennings
Lady Else; beautiful Else,

My own experience
You will rarely find a service tree standing on its own as they prefer the company of other trees in the forest. It has an extremely hard wood, and in its essential nature is related to all sorbus species (sorb, whitebeam, rowan). Cheerful, fundamentally solid, and robust, it does not seek for solitude but joyfully contributes its part in the family of the wood.

It acts resolutely and decidedly to counter grousing, spiritlessness and queasy feelings in the stomach and below, ensuring that any such will be excreted promptly. Hence in the Middle Ages it was used as a medicine for dysentery!

It is a tree with which any woman and any man can converse when they have problems how to be real self-respecting masculine man respectively a self-esteeming, feminine woman. Kind Lady Else will get them back on track, with a cheerful laugh and a few affectionate, if necessary hard slaps. 'Kind understanding cooperation and partnership instead of silly competition is the key!'

Notes
Martin Luther's wife evidently ate the berries on a massive scale which permits us to speculate on this former nuns congenial being. Lucky Martin...

For a clever forester the tree could be a prolific source of income, for a litre of 'Adelitzenbrand' spirit can be sold for several hundred euros, and the wood commands top prices for veneering, or for sounding boards in instrument making, flutes or organ pipes!

Spruce, Norway spruce, European spruce
Picea abies

Kennings
Loudest moan; the begin of an answer or call; confidence in spring; courage; faith; peace; security; protection and warmth in winter; cool distance; straightness; warming mother of the mountains

My own experience
If you need motherly counsel and comfort, talk to a spruce. As a very powerful ancient female tree, the spruce dispenses balsamic comfort all year round. It is a motherly friend of all those who want to be carried in the arms of the Great Mother. It is there all year round for those who approach it. The cares and pains of life vanish in the murmur of the wind through its branches. It has a balancing effect, cooling in summer, warming in winter. Its hanging cones are a further indication of its motherly powers, which can be felt flowing very strongly underneath the spruce's branches. The centre of gravity and main strength of the spruce are in its crown. If the crown breaks, the tree recovers only with difficulty.

Be careful if you fancy the idea of letting yourself be rocked by the wind in the crown of the tree. Spruce branches are hurt by hard soles of shoes, and moreover a fall can have fatal consequences. In Summer but especially in winter, the consciousness residing in its trunk can clearly be felt just sitting at its foot.

Although being very empathic, the spruce is not sentimental at all. Branches near the base which serve no kind of useful purpose are given up and wither, in favour of branches higher up which get more sunlight. It is much the same with things, habits and acquaintances in our life.

Note
All conifers embody the motherly aspect in whatever form. The spruce is one of the strongest of these avatars. In artificial monocultures, however, this aspect tips over into an oppressive darkness and acidified soil. Like a convent of vitriolic ladies.

Strawberry tree
Arbutus spp.

Kennings
Friend of birds, lizards and walkers all the same.

My own experience
Its large yellow berries (later turning orange, red and finally black) are a 'hearty and healthy snack for walkers along the way'.

Never mind how hard and laborious our winding road of life may seem, whether we move ahead purposefully or wander around without direction, the arbutus or strawberry tree always brings us to a cheerful pause. Its fruits simply gleam too enticing, and they taste much to delicious to just pass them by.

With the colour of its berries the strawberry tree shows us that life consists of three major ages: youth, maturity and age. Each age has a beauty of its own – the gleam of youth, full maturity with all its power, and age with its contentment and spiritual ripeness.

Every age has its own possibilities, only accessible at that time. When you deliberately make use of these possibilities, the power of the arbutus reveals to you the beauty of your own path, wherever it may be headed for. Luck waits for the ones prepared for and embracing it.

Note
The entire maquis of Corsica is thick with arbutus trees (A. unedo). In the rest of Europe, they are unknown to me. But they are said to occur in Mediterranean regions and from California down to Nicaragua (A. menziesii et al.). Perhaps this is a further reason for the cheerful Mediterranean and West Coast temperament?

Sweet chestnut, edible chestnut, maroni tree
Castanea sativa

Kennings
Prickles; helps with angry temper; wise foresight; bread tree
hard bread; good for the lonely; tree of cheerful togetherness
comfortable and secure

My own experience
As a friend of the jay, the squirrel, the dormouse, the crow and the pig,
it returned with the Greeks and Romans to the southern regions of
Europe after the last Ice Age. Not so bitter as the fruit of the horse-
chestnut, the edible chestnut prickles you with thousands of fine
needles, which in addition to their leather-penetrating sharpness
break off easily in the wound. In chestnut groves, these prickly balls
cover the ground everywhere.

Its history is intertwined with the hard destiny of poor people living
in the Ticino, who were obliged to mix their flour with chestnut flour
in order to be able to bake bread at all. Clever peasants, especially in
the Ticino, therefore planted entire groves of chestnut trees in their
wise foresight, as a resource for times of scarcity. It is said that two
'maroni-trees' can feed one man for a whole year. – What a hard and
toilsome bread! And yet, what a good thing to act with foresight in
good time. - Concerning both: hard times of need, and the spikes.

A quite different aspect relates to intimate togetherness under the
maroni tree, or when eating chestnuts. For all those who are receptive,
who listen carefully, the sweet chestnut can awake the sexual drive in
a cheerful and humorous way. With the same energy, it mitigates
anger caused by the stinging injustices of this world, and like this
directs the perspective to life's beautiful possibilities. The lonely
among us may time after time find consolation and new faith experiencing its easy and yet persistent cheerfulness, as well as feeling a
quiet sense of comfort and security in themselves.
Just like the chestnut in its husk.

Swiss pine, arolla pine, stone pine,
Pinus cembra

Kennings
The tree of the Alps; avalanche-bane; friend of the nutcracker and the squirrel; twisty (contorted growth); cools in summer and warms in winter; cool head and warm feet; adaptable; relaxation; endurance; strength of will; persistence; leisureliness; gentle peace in the heights.

My own experience
The tree is very flexible and adapts its form of growth easily to outward conditions. A widely branching root system and a good network of root fungi also help the arolla to anchor itself effectively. For this reason too it is very enduring and steadfast. No matter how the weather may be raging, it will always have warm feet! The arolla is the home of the good little pinefolk. You also have an opportunity here to sense or very rarely encounter powerful mountain spirits like venerable Grandmaster Rübezahl.

In the rustling of the arolla pine we can realize how unimportant our own problems are. The arolla mends inner and outer disruption. The Swiss pine can resolve stubborn physical and spiritual cramps. It rewards the pure in heart, and sometimes plays nasty tricks on the greedy. 'Be honest, true and upright' then or suffer often rather earthy practical jokes. 'Leave all attachment behind. Be compassionate – stay like this and feel the liberating consequences of your own benediction.'

Notes
As a cough syrup, or when rubbed in as a rheumatism oil, it has a healing effect on chronic and acute conditions resulting from invasions by cold. For people with cold feet or with gout, this is the tree of choice. The only precondition for experiencing its healing effect is the willingness to let go, deliberately let yourself drop into peace and regeneration. Pineclad rooms or pine furniture, give an incredible amount of warmth and shelter to those who know how to appreciate it.

Tulip tree, tulip or yellow poplar, canoewood, saddle-leaf tree, white wood
Líridendron tulipifera

Kennings
Tree of lights; The blossoms of peace; carpe diem; peaceful tree; ahimsa; warmth in summer and autumn

My own experience
The tulip tree was reintroduced from America, having died out in Europe in the last Ice Age. As a result, you will find the tulip tree most commonly in parks.

With its wonderfully beautiful big white flowers, which gleam like a thousand radiant candles, and its rainproof roof of big green leaves, in summer it suggests uplifted sublime thoughts of elves and carefree confidence in the warm sunshine. The forest-dwelling Native Americans recognised this and liked to build their hunting platforms and tree houses under its thick crown of leaves. They also used its light wood to make canoes.

At the start of autumn its leaves take on a gleaming yellow hue. Even in the face of coming winter, the tree radiates a power of illumination that is unparalleled. Once winter has arrived, the tulip tree accepts it, sheds its leaves and withdraws into sleep. During winter, its very transpicuous branch structure is a notable feature. Therefore, the tree is not much at risk of having its branches broken by snow.

It does not deny the winter of life but encourages us to accept the beautiful things gratefully for as long as they last. If you are a friend of the elves and want to learn peaceable intentions as the highest form of self-perfection, visit a tulip tree. Like some sage Native American Indians, it knows the secret of the invincible power of the peaceful heart.

Notes
It may be that a very known but copyrighted fantasy author drew inspiration from the tulip tree, with its radiant blossoms, its yellow autumn leaves and bright bark, for his vision of elvish tree-dwellings.

Unknown tree

Arbor ignotus

Kennings
The stranger; surprise; new experience

My own experience
Many tree-lovers have a personal relationship with one special tree. Some in fact have contact only with 'their' tree. But the woods and many arboretums offer a variety of new, sometimes completely unexpected encounters of an exciting and inspiring nature.

For beginners though, practising just with one tree of your acquaintance, one that likes you, can be a more sensible approach than storming into the wood and treading on the roots of another tree every five minutes.

First take a full look at the tree. Try to apprehend its shape, seize, logic of branching and try to sense its whole being, then gently approach, and let yourself be surprised. As long as a tree's growth has not been seriously thwarted, and it does not present a clearly threatening aspect, you need have no fear of approaching it.[36]

Just let yourself be drawn. Don't try to force anything and listen attentively with all your senses and bring your imagination in resonance with the tree. Just be open for anything that may come.

Note
I would be delighted to hear about your experiences with trees. Just send me a report to info@druidenwissen.de. Even if they are deeply individual, I can gain a more multifaceted picture of the individual trees by collocating the different experiences.

---

[36] Except in severe weather of course: 'Cave Caput, Ligna Cadunt!'

Willow, Sallow
Salix spp.

Kennings
Sally tree; bees joy; origin of honey; the bending; gentle healing; stunning the pain; peaceful; Demeter's tree; rebirth and renewal

My own experience
The willow is the companion of flowing water. From the happily sputtering mountain creek to the serene stream, its energies are crucially determined by the water in its vicinity. It often even takes root in water.

It brings forgetfulness of cares, tensions and pains, just as if these were being gently carried away on the flowing stream. Like practically no other tree it is capable of healing pain and even wounds of the soul. It often dispenses its motherly counsel through dreams, if you doze or sleep underneath it.

A healthy willow, by which we can linger for a brief space and have a rest from the exhausting troubles of everyday, is a relaxing companion in the stream of life. If you enjoy sitting by the water, sit down in the shade of a healthy willow and let yourself be gently lulled into a refreshing sleep. But be careful: A willow next to flowing water is often a deeply melancholic tree, that can evoke melancholy and almost narcotic drowsiness in some people, especially on hot summer days. And be advised to exercise caution or best avoid crippled or half withered willows. Those can indeed stalk your awareness and lure you into an energy-sapping stupefaction.

Notes
The willow is a pioneer tree. It is an amazing survivor and, with the exception of the brittle or crack willow, very flexible. Its bark yields salicin, which was used in former times as an anaesthetic in all kinds of situations. As is so often the case, the concentrated, purely chemical form of the substance, torn out of its operative plant base, has serious side-effects.

Yew
Taxus spp.

Kennings
Most honourable of all trees; World Tree of the Celts;
Golden Fleece (pollen); deepest wisdom; solemn comfort; long life
and mortality; life and death; archery (yeomen); food of lepers

My own experience
This is a very serious, unbelievably wise tree, versed in the deepest
mysteries. The yew is a solemn and fair counsellor even in times of
profound despair or with the most important questions of life.

To the wise yew, wandering between the worlds, whether in meditation, or after death is very familiar. As it encompasses wisdom found
through wandering times and realms, it can help even in the most
serious crises of life, in the loss or death of people you love and other
finally terminal situations, enabling you to survive and/or find a new
beginning. In the gloomiest valley it provides a glimmer of hope,
which will develop into unshakeable trust in life.

Even in the darkest depths of winter it holds onto its needles and
offers its fruit as food to the birds. With its red 'berries' It even shines
like a Christmas tree. It gives us the certainty that every winter will be
followed by a spring. A new spring in which it releases its yellow-gold
pollen into the warm spring sun, like a golden fleece. Finding protection and regaining faith in situations which may often appear impossible for us to comprehend – that is the power, consolation and the
comfort of the yew.

Notes
Normally yews and children do not go well together, because all parts
of it, apart from the flesh of the seed (but even including the kernel of
the seed), are deadly poisonous. If you want to eat a berry, remove the
kernel by hand first. It does not look nice, but else you might die. Yews
are deadly serious!! Even its pollen is allergenic.

List of references
Just a selection: True wisdom is to be found at the foot of a tree...

Awaken Healing Light of the Tao: *(1993) Mantak & Maneewan Chia, Healing Tao Books*

Bäume der Welt [Trees of the World], Oxford Enyklopädie [Oxford Encyclopaedia]: *(1998) Bayard Hora, DRW-Verlag*

Bäume und Sträucher des Waldes [Trees and Shrubs of the World]: *(1984) Gottfried Ammann, Neumann Verlag*

Baumheilkunde: Heilkraft, Mythos und Magie der Bäume [Healing Art of Trees; Healing Powers, Myth and Magic of the Trees]: *(2008) Renato Strassmann, Knaur*

Baummagie [Tree Magic]: *(2001) Steve Blamires, Hugendubel, Munich*

Blätter von Bäumen [Leaves of Trees]: *(2001) Susanne Fischer-Rizzi, 10th edition, Irisiana, Munich*

Botschaft der Bäume [Message of the Trees]: *(2000) Dietmar Findling, Kosmos, Stuttgart*

Chrut und Uchrut [Herbs and Weeds]: *(1917) Fr Johann Künzle, no details given*

Das Chakra Aura System [The Chakra Aura System]: *(2007) Wiwi R. Raupach Hochheim 2007*

Das Chakra-Handbuch [The Chakra Manual]: *(1999) S.Sharamon, B.Baginski 43rd edition, Windpferd, Aitrang*

Das grosse Kräuterheilbuch [The Big Book of Herbal Remedies]: *(2006) Fr Johann Künzle, new edition published by Walter Verlag*

Das grosse Praxisbuch der Baumheilkunde [The Big Practical Manual of the Healing Art of Trees] (...): *(2006) Doris and Sven Richter, Aquamarin*

Der alte Pfad Wege zur Natur in uns selbst [The Ancient Path – Ways to Find Nature in Ourselves]: *(2010) Vicky Gabriel, Arun Verlag*

Der Garten der Druiden [The Garden of the Druids]: *(2008) Claudia Urbanowsky, Ullstein*

Der germanische Götterhimmel [The Germanic Pantheon]: *(2009) Voenix, Arun-Verlag*

Der Stadt-Schamane [The Urban Shaman]: *(1991) Serge Kahili-King, Lüchow*

Der Weg des Schamanen [The Way of the Shaman]: *(2004) Michael Harner, Ullstein*

Die Druiden: Mythos, Magie und Wirklichkeit der Kelten [The Druids: Myth, Magic and Reality of the Celts]: *(2006) F. LeRoux C. J. Guyonvarch, Arun-Verlag*

Die Edda des Snorri Sturluson: Göttererzählungen und Gedichte [The Edda of Snorri Sturluson: Stories of the Gods and Poems]: *(1997) Arnulf Krause, Reclam*

Die Eibe in neuem Licht [The Yew in a New Light]: *(2007) Fred Hageneder, Neue Erde, Saarbrücken*

Die Götter und Heldenlieder der älteren Edda [The Gods and Songs of Heroes in the Elder Edda]: (2004) *Arnulf Krause, Reclam*

Die grossen Sagen der Welt [The Great Sagas of the World]: *(1968) H. Eich / A. Provensen / M. Provensen, O. Maier-Verlag*

Die Kraft des Ortes: Die Energien der Erde erspüren, erkennen und nutzen [The Power of the Place: Sensing, Recognising and Using the Energies of the Earth]: *(2009) Stefan Brönnle, Neue Erde*

Die Kräuterkunde des Paracelsus: Therapie mit Heilpflanzen nach abendländischer Tradition [The Herbal Lore of Paracelsus: Therapy with Healing Plants, based on the Occidental Tradition]: *(2006) O. Rippe / M. Madejisky, AT-Verlag*

Die magische Welt der Kelten [The Magical World of the Celts]: *(2002) Ansha, Ludwig*

Die spirituellen Kräfte der Bäume [The Spiritual Powers of Trees] *(1999): Petra Sonnenberg, Iris, Amsterdam*

Druiden: Die Weisheit der Kelten [Druids: The Wisdom of the Celts]: *(2009) J. L. Brunaux / S. Held, Klett-Cota*

Einheimische Bäume und Sträucher [Native Trees and Shrubs]: *(2004) Jean-Denis Godet, Haymarket Media*

Geist der Bäume [Spirit of the Trees] *(2000): Fred Hageneder, 2nd edition, Neue Erde, Saarbrücken*

Germanische Götter und Heldensagen [German Gods and Sagas of the Heroes] *(2004): Felix and Therese Dahn, Marixverlag*

Gesundheit, Vitalität und langes Leben [Health, Vitality and Long Life] (1996): *Mantak Chia, Heyne*

Götter und Helden der Wikinger [Gods and Heroes of the Vikings]: *(1995) B. Branston / G. Caselli, Tessloff*

Heilkunde: Das Buch von dem Grund und Wissen und der Heilung der Krankheiten [Healing Lore: the Book of the Cause, Knowledge and Healing of Diseases]: *(1992) Hildegard v. Bingen, new edition published by Otto Müller Verlag*

Illias und Odyssee [Iliad and Odyssey]: *(2002) Homer, translated by J.H. Voss, DTV*

Kahuna-Magie - Das Wissen um eine weise Lebensführung [Kahuna Magic – the Art of Wise Living]: *(2004) Max Freedom Long, Schirner*

Keltische Weisheitsstäbchen. Ein Ogam-Orakel [Celtic Wisdom Sticks – an Ogham Oracle]: *(2002) Caitilin Matthews, Kailash*

König Arthur und die Ritter der Tafelrunde [King Arthur and the Knights of the Round Table]: *Sir Thomas Malory (2009), Anaconda*

Kosmos-Baumführer Europa: 680 Bäume, 2600 Zeichnungen [Kosmos Guide to European Trees: 680 Trees, 2600 Illustrations]: *(2011) Margot and Roland Spohn, Frankh-Kosmos*

Le Manuscrit des Paroles du Druide Sans Nom et Sans Visage [The Manuscript of the Words of the Druid Without Name and Without Face]: *(1996) Emmanuel-Yves Monin, publisher unknown*

Magische Welt der Kelten: Die Weisheit der Druiden und Barden [Magical World of the Celts: the Wisdom of the Druids and Bards] *(2005), Gondolino, no publishing details given*

Mythos Baum [The Myth of the Tree]: *(2000) Doris Laudert, Blv*

Naturpfade: Spiritualität & Ritual im Alltag [Nature Paths: Spirituality & Ritual in Everday Living]: *(2005) V.Gabriel / W. Anderson, Arun*

Pflanzen der Kelten: Heilkunde, Pflanzenzauber, Baumkalender [Plants of the Celts: Healing Lore, Plant Magic, Tree Calendar]: *(2000) Wolf-Dieter Storl, AT-Verlag*

Pflanzendevas: Die geistig-seelischen Dimensionen der Pflanzen [Plant Devas: the Spiritual-Soul Dimensions of Plants]: *(2010) Wolf-Dieter Storl, Knaur*

Quest: In Search of the Dragontooth: *(1994) Michael Green, Running Press Books*

'Tao Yoga' series *(various) Mantak and Manneewan Chia, Ansata*

The Book of Druidry, 2nd Edition: History, Sites and Wisdom: *(1992) Ross Nichols, Thorsons*

The Mabinogion: *(1976) Anonymous / Jeffrey Gantz, Penguin Classics*

The Way of Hermes (…): *(2001) Hermes Trismegistus, (translated by Oyen, Mahe et al.), Gerald Duckworth &Co*

Welcher Baum ist das? [What Kind of Tree is That?]: *(2009) Joachim Mayer, Kosmos*

Weltenesche Eschenwelten: Das germanische Götterorakel und Nachschlagewerk [World Ash / Ash Worlds: the Germanic Oracle of the Gods and Reference Work]: *(2001) Voenix, Arun*

Zauners Laubbäume-Kompass [Zauner's Vade Mecum for Deciduous Trees] (…): *(publishing date unknown) Georg Zauner, Gräfe und Unzer*